Ancient history from the monuments

Greek cities & islands of Asia Minor

W. S. W. Vaux

Alpha Editions

This edition published in 2024

ISBN : 9789366381053

Design and Setting By
Alpha Editions
www.alphaedis.com
Email - info@alphaedis.com

As per information held with us this book is in Public Domain.
This book is a reproduction of an important historical work. Alpha Editions uses the best technology to reproduce historical work in the same manner it was first published to preserve its original nature. Any marks or number seen are left intentionally to preserve its true form.

CHAPTER I.
INTRODUCTION.

Cyzicus—Lampsacus—Abydus—Assus—Palæ-Scepsis—Troy—Dr. Schliemann—Ilium Novum—Alexandria—Troas—Pergamum or Pergamus—Æolis.

BEFORE we proceed to give a somewhat detailed account of the more important cities of Asia Minor, and of the islands adjacent to its west and southern shores, we may mention that Asia Minor, as it lies on the map, exhibits, in its contour, a remarkable resemblance to Spain. Extending between N. Lat. 36° and 42°, and E. Long. 26° and 40°, it is about the same size as France, and somewhat less than Spain and Portugal taken together. Its interior consists of a central plateau, rarely lower than 3,000 ft. above the sea, often much more; many portions of it, however, especially to the N. and E., affording excellent pasturage for sheep, and, therefore, now, as for centuries, the natural home of the Turkomán shepherds.

At the S.W. end of Asia Minor terminates, also, the great central mountain-range of Asia itself, which, running from the Brahmaputra westwards, connects the Himálayas and the Caucasus.

Many of the streams flowing from these mountains are heavily charged with lime; hence the remarkable deposits of travertine, &c., to be seen at Hierapolis and elsewhere. Indeed, to the geological features of the country we owe the fact that the military and commercial routes through Asia Minor have been always nearly the same, the earliest and the latest conquerors having followed the same roads.

The present produce of Asia Minor is almost insignificant when considered with reference to its geographical area, and to the great wealth extracted from it by the Romans (Cic. pro Leg. Manil. 2). But every land, alike, decays under the oppressive and unintelligent rule of the Osmanlis of Constantinople. The name, Asia Minor, we may add, is comparatively modern, and is not met with earlier than Orosius, in the fifth century A.D., while that of Anatolia (Ἀνατολή) is used first by Constantinus Porphyrogenitus, in the tenth century A.D.

The chief provinces of Asia Minor (omitting the smaller subdivisions of Ionia, Æolis, and Troas, included, as these latter are usually, under Mysia and Lydia) are the following:—Mysia, Lydia, Caria, to the W., and fronting the Ægean Sea; Lycia, Pamphylia, and Cilicia, opposite to Crete and Cyprus; Bithynia, Paphlagonia, and Pontus, on the Black Sea; and, in the centre, Pisidia and Lycaonia, Phrygia, Galatia and Cappadocia.

We propose to notice the more important towns, according to the order of the provinces just recited; and, following this order, we take first Mysia and its chief town, CYZICUS (the *Esquize* of mediæval times), which was situated on the neck of a peninsula running out into the Sea of Marmora. Mr. Hamilton describes its position as "a sandy isthmus, having near its southern end many large blocks of stone," not, improbably, the remains of Strabo's "bridge." Many ancient monuments may still be traced among its present cherry-orchards, attesting its original magnitude and magnificence, most of the relics now visible being Roman, and its destruction having, no doubt, been mainly due to the great earthquakes in the reign of Tiberius and Aurelius, which ruined and depopulated so many other of the fairest towns of Asia Minor.[1]

> 1. Tacitus, speaking of A.D. 17, the 4th of Tiberius, says:—"Eodem anno duodecim celebres Asiæ urbes collapsæ nocturno motu terræ" (Annal. ii. c. 47): and Cicero speaks of Cyzicus as "urbem Asiæ celeberrimam nobisque amicissimam." Compare also Apoll. Rhod. i. 936-941, 983-987; Valer. Max. ii. 630; Ovid. Trist. i. 9.

Mr. Hamilton, indeed, noting the loose and rubbly character of its buildings, doubts the architectural fame of the city; but it is probable that what we now see was once cased with marble, as much fine marble is found in the adjacent hills. Some, too, of its buildings are of a granite easily disintegrable. Any how, it would seem to be a place where well-conducted excavations might bring to light many curious relics of the past. Cyzicus was classed by Anaximenes of Lampsacus among the colonies of Miletus, but was not of importance till the close of the Peloponnesian war, when, by the discreditable peace of Antalcidas, it was surrendered to the Persians, its ultimate prosperity being in great measure due to its position, as a natural entrepôt, between the Black Sea and the Ægean. In Roman times it was, according to Strabo, a "Libera civitas," and, with the exception of Nicomedia and Nicæa, the most important city in that part of Asia Minor. In the days of Caracalla it had become a "Metropolis," and, still later, was an Episcopal see.

Of the great wealth and, we may perhaps add, of the popularity of its citizens in the fifth and fourth century B.C., the gold coins, called Cyzicene *staters*, are ample evidence; though it may be doubted whether, as was once thought, the *zecchino* (or sequin), means *Cyzicene*. In an able paper by Dr. (now Sir Patrick) Colquhoun (Trans. Roy. Liter. vol. iv. p. 35), it is clearly shown that the "*Squise*" of Ville-Hardouin is the ancient Cyzicus, "the oldest commercial place in the world," as that writer, with some exaggeration, asserts. The form "Esquisse" is probably, as Dr. Colquhoun suggests, a corruption of εἰς Κύζικον ("to Cyzicus").[2] Dr. Colquhoun's paper is full of curious information on the early mediæval state of this part of Asia Minor. Its decline was mainly due to the invasion of the Goths in A.D. 262, but it long remained the metropolis of the Hellespontine province (Hierocl. Synecd. p. 661. Malala, Chron. i. p. 364). It was finally destroyed by an earthquake in A.D. 943.

2. Similar modern modifications may be noticed in other sites of the Levant. Thus, Stanchio (Kos) comes from εἰς τήν Κῶν; Stamboul is not, necessarily, a corruption of Constantinopolis, but, more probably, of εἰς τήν πόλιν ("to the city"); so Stalimene (Lesbos) comes from εἰς τόν λιμένα ("to the port").

Another Mysian town of note was LAMPSACUS, also a colony of Miletus and Phocæa, attested as this is by its gold and silver coins, and by a statue of a prostrate lion, said to have been the work of Lysippus, and subsequently, placed by Agrippa in the Campus Martius at Rome. The town was famous for its wine, and was, for this reason, granted to Themistocles, who is said to have learnt here, or at Magnesia, Persian in a year; the district around having been granted to him by his old enemy the King of Persia. Like most of the towns of western Asia Minor, it often changed hands during the rival contests of its more powerful neighbours; but, having, with a wise forethought, voted a crown of gold to the Romans, it was accepted by them as an ally,[3] and, hence, was, in the time of Strabo, a town of some magnitude. A small village, called Lampsaki, most likely marks on our modern maps the site of the old town.

3. Liv. xliii. 6. Most likely, its brave resistance to Antiochus had favourably inclined the Romans to it (Liv. xxxiii. 38; xxxv. 42; Polyb. xxi. 10).

A little to the south of Lampsacus was ABYDUS, at the narrowest part of the Hellespont, and opposite the town of Sestus.[4] It was a little above Abydus that Xerxes constructed his famous bridge, B.C. 480; but, except for the gallant resistance it made to Philip, son of Demetrius, king of Macedon, Abydus has no place in history. In legendary lore, however, it was the scene of the famous swimming of Leander to visit his lady-love, the Priestess of the Temple at Sestus, on the opposite or European shore, a natatory feat, however, far surpassed in recent days. Lord Byron's lines on the subject are well known:—

He could, perhaps, have pass'd the Hellespont,

As once (a feat on which ourselves we prided)

Leander, Mr. Ekenhead, and I did.

Don Juan, Cant. ii. 105.

4. The average breadth of the Hellespont was about three miles—rather narrow for Homer's πλατύς, "the broad." He, probably, however, looked on it rather as a mighty river; to which, indeed, his epithets of ἀγάρροος and ἀπείρων ("strong-flowing," and "boundless") well enough apply. Herodotus calls it δολερός and ἁλμυρός ποταμός, "a treacherous and unsavoury river" (vii. 35).

Leander's labour, however, was greater than that of the poet or his companion, in that he swam *against* the stream to reach Sestus, the current being often so powerful that a well-manned boat cannot be pulled straight across it.

A little further down the coast, and facing nearly due south, is ASSUS, a site which has been visited by many travellers, as Walpole, Choiseul-Gouffier, Raoul-Rochette, Fellows, and Pullan. The most ancient monuments of Greek art in the Louvre at Paris were removed thence. The position of the chief buildings is very grand; indeed, in Strabo's time, Assus was considered as a fortress almost inaccessible.[5] Its ruins are still remarkably perfect, one gate at least, of triangular construction, resembling those at Mycenæ and Arpinum. There are, also, vestiges of a hexastyle Doric temple, showing some analogy with those at Pæstum. Seventeen large fragments from the metopes and two façades of the Temple were ultimately removed to France by Capt. Chaigneau, together with a Doric capital. They were found scattered over the slope of the hill, and must have been removed at some time or the other, probably for building purposes; indeed, fragments of similar pieces were also noticed in some of the neighbouring houses. In character of workmanship, the sculptures resemble the Æginetan marbles now at the British Museum. But their execution is not so effective, the material of which they are made being the coarse red stone of the neighbourhood. To the same cause is, perhaps, due the fact that they had not been carried away long ago. Had they been of fine marble, they would have been valuable plunder. Sir Charles Fellows, speaking of Assus, says, "After depositing my baggage, I took the most intelligent Turk in the place as my cicerone.... Immediately around me were the ruins, extending for miles, undisturbed by any living creature except the goats and kids. On every side lay columns, triglyphs and friezes, of beautiful sculpture, every object speaking of the grandeur of this ancient city. In one place I saw thirty Doric capitals placed up in a line for a fence." Sir Charles Fellows gives a drawing of one of the friezes now in Paris, and adds, "I then entered the Via Sacra, or Street of Tombs, extending for miles. Some of these tombs still stand in their original beautiful forms, but most have been opened, and the lids are lying near the walls they covered, curiosity or avarice having been satisfied by displacing them.... These ruins are on a considerably larger scale than those of the Roman city, and many of the remains are equally perfect. Several are highly ornamented and have inscriptions; others are as large as a temple, being twenty to thirty feet square; the usual height of the sarcophagus is from ten to twelve feet."[6]

<u>5</u>. The character of the position of Assus led to a joke of the musician Stratonicus, who applied to it a line of Homer (Il. vii. 144), playing on the meaning of the word Ἆσσον, viz.

Ἆσσον ἴθ', ὡς κεν θᾶσσον ὀλέθρου πείραθ' ἵκηαι,

Come more quickly (or come to Assus), "that ye may the more quickly come to utter destruction." At Assus, St. Luke, and other companions of St. Paul, rejoined him with their ship, the Apostle having walked on foot from Alexandria Troas (Acts xx. 13).

<u>6</u>. The popular story of the "Lapis Assius," with its supposed power of destroying the flesh of bodies buried in it (whence the name *sarkophagus*, or "flesh-consuming,") is noticed by Dioskorides and Pliny. But this Greek word is rarely used for a tomb, the more usual word being σορός (soros). By the Romans, however, it was used, as in Juv. x. 170. Colonel Leake observes of the ruins of Assos, "The whole gives, perhaps, the most perfect idea of a Greek city that anywhere exists" (Asia Minor, p. 128). See also R. P. Pullan, "Ruins of Asia Minor," p. 19.

PALÆ-SCEPSIS is interesting for the native tradition, that it was once the capital of Æneas's dominions. It appears to have been situated near the source of the Æsepus—high up on Mount Ida—the later Scepsis being about sixty stadia (7½ miles) lower down (Strabo, xiii. 607). Dr. Colquhoun[7] states that a village in the neighbourhood still bears the name of *Eski Skisepje*, which, as Eski means "old" in Turkish, corresponds with Palæ-Scepsis; Dr. Colquhoun at the same time quotes the words of its discoverer, the distinguished Oriental scholar, Dr. Mordtmann. "I did discover," says Dr. Mordtmann, "a most ancient city with its acropolis, towers and walls built of hewn stone, and furnished with four gates. The antiquity of the place was manifested by an oak having fixed its roots in the wall, and by its trunk having grown to a girth of 530 centimètres (about 17 feet). On reference to Strabo, I first became aware that I had discovered, probably, the most ancient ruin in Asia Minor, for I hold that this can be no other than Palæ-Scepsis." The evidence adduced by Drs. Mordtmann and Colquhoun confirms the accuracy of Strabo. The later town of Scepsis is memorable for the discovery there, during the time of Sylla, of the works of Aristotle and Theophrastus, which had been buried by the illiterate relations of one Neleus (a pupil of Aristotle and friend of Theophrastus), lest they should be carried off by Attalus, then founding his library at Pergamus. It appears from Strabo, that though preserved from utter ruin, the precious MSS. had suffered much from damp and worms; but they suffered still more by the injudicious efforts of their purchaser, Apellicon of Teos, a well-meaning person, though wholly incompetent to supply the gaps he found.

> 7. See Dr. Colquhoun "On the Site of the Palæ-Scepsis of Strabo" (Trans. R. S. Liter., vol. iv. 1852).

But the most celebrated place in Mysia was the ancient city of TROY. It would be out of place here, indeed impossible, to discuss any of the various theories of ancient or modern times referring to this famous town and its no less famous war. It is enough to state here our firm belief in the existence of both, and further, that the legends since grouped around them by no means demand any such non-existence. We have no doubt that a prominent conical hill, now called Hissarlik, does represent the spot where old Troy once stood.[8] The convergency of the various stories of ancient history, the existence at Hissarlik of ruins of remote antiquity, and the singular fitness of the position (unless, indeed, all that is attributed to Homer is to be condemned as purely mythical), lead to the seemingly inevitable conclusion that here, if anywhere, once stood this celebrated town.

> 8. It has been, justly, we think, remarked (Quarterly Review, April, 1874), that "not one of the sceptical critics has ever questioned that these (the Homeric poems) show an acquaintance with the topography of the region which (and this is no small point) has borne, from all known antiquity, the name of the Troad.... Homer's Ida, and Scamander, and Hellespont are as real in his pages as in their existence at the present day."

The inhabitants of Ilium were a mixed population, partly, it is probable, of Thracian origin, and so far only Greek that a Pelasgian element may be traced in both peoples, while they were probably, also, inferior in civilization to the Greeks, with barbaric habits and manners, already obsolete among their more polished enemies. Nor, again, is it at all necessary to maintain that the capture of Troy implies its entire destruction; it is, indeed, more likely that its ultimate ruin was due to the enmity of its Asiatic neighbours, as suggested by Strabo on the authority of an ancient writer, Xanthus. It is clear that Ilium stood on rising ground, between the rivers Scamander and Simois, and that here were placed the palaces of Priam and of his sons. The whole spot was, we may reasonably conclude, surrounded by strong walls, with many gates, only one of which is, however, noticed in Homer by name. Such was the tradition, the long endurance of which is shown in the subsequent sacrifice by Xerxes, recorded by Herodotus (vii. 43).

The new Ilium of later days most likely occupied the same traditional site; the theory of Demetrius of Scepsis, adopted by Strabo, of two Iliums separated the one from the other by a considerable interval of ground, being clearly adverse to a common-sense view of the question.[9] Any one would naturally expect that those who constructed *Novum Ilium* would select that place for their town to which the legends most distinctly pointed; while a manifest objection to the view of Demetrius is that it converts Homer from a poet into a topographer, and attempts to make the natural features of the country accord with his poetic descriptions. It is far more probable that Homer, or whoever collected the poems passing under his name, had but a very general idea of the localities where were laid the scenes he describes: while there is, also, no general agreement as to the true site of Troy among those writers who, in modern times, have more or less accepted the theory of Demetrius and Strabo. Indeed, on the idea of Homer having written his poems with an Ordnance map in his lap, it is simply impossible to fix on any one spot that satisfies all the conditions of his story.

> 9. The site for ancient Ilium of recent years the most popular is called *Bournarbashi*, where the Scamander emerges from the lower ridges of Mount Ida, and, therefore, not far from the "village of the Ilians." This view, proposed originally by Chevallier in 1788, and, subsequently, adopted by Rennell, Leake, Welckher, Forchhammer, Choiseul-Gouffier, and others, has, however, been completely answered by Grote, whose arguments have been fully confirmed by the latest researches.

We must now notice the recent marvellous researches of Dr. Schliemann, for, though they have done little towards the revelation of Homer's Troy, they have demonstrated that, many feet below very ancient and still existing walls, there have once been enormous structures, the treasury, fortress, and royal residence of some wealthy ruler of remote antiquity. While, therefore, we do not believe that Dr. Schliemann has found old Troy, in the same sense that Layard discovered the palaces of Sardanapalus, the Greek inscriptions he has unearthed have assuredly proved the identity of the modern Hissarlik with *Novum* Ilium. What, then, is the history of Schliemann's researches, and what has he done that any other man might not have done with as ample means at his command? Doubtless there are other men who might have done as much as he, notably Mr. Layard. As Dr. Schliemann was much influenced by his early education at home, and as his career has been a very extraordinary one, we feel sure our readers would like to know something of the digger as well of as what he has dug out. We purpose, therefore, to give a brief sketch of his personal history, and then, with equal brevity, to add a notice of what he has accomplished.

Born in 1822 at a small village in Mecklenburg, he tells us that, "as soon as I learnt to speak my father related to me the great deeds of the Homeric heroes," and, though from ten years of age he was an apprentice in a warehouse,[10] he always retained, as he adds, "the same love for the famous men of antiquity which I conceived for them in my first childhood." As time went on Schliemann became a clerk, though on a yearly salary of only £32: but he contrived to live on half—to do without a fire, and to devote all his spare moments to the study of languages. Thus he learnt first English and French, each in six months, and then other modern tongues, including Russ.

> <u>10</u>. In this "warehouse," let it not be forgotten, Schliemann was employed from fourteen to twenty years of age, from 5 A.M. to 11 P.M., selling herrings, butter, brandy, milk, &c.; and that it was not till after he had lost this occupation from an injury caused by lifting a cask, that he was *promoted* to the clerkship at the salary mentioned in the text.

To Dutch, Spanish, Italian, and Portuguese he allowed only six weeks each. During the eight years from 1846 to 1854 he was so much occupied in business that he had no time for literature; in the latter end, however, of the second year he found time to learn Swedish and Polish. It was not till January, 1856, that he ventured to attack Greek, his fear being, as he naïvely remarks, that the fascination of its study might interfere with his commercial duties. Aided however by two Greek friends, he tells us he learnt modern Greek in six weeks, and, in three months more, sufficient classical Greek to understand the ancient writers, and especially Homer. In 1858 Dr. Schliemann was able to travel over Sweden, Denmark, Germany, Italy, and Egypt, on the way learning somewhat of (we presume colloquial) Arabic, and returning thence through Syria and Athens to St. Petersburg. It was not, however, till 1863 that he had secured, by his vigorous commercial occupations, the means to spend the rest of his life as he pleased.

His first plan, in 1864, was to visit the fatherland of Ulysses, but this was only a hasty and flying trip, and he was, shortly afterwards, induced to extend his journey to India, China, and Japan. On his return to Europe he spent some time in Paris, but made also, thence, journeys to Greece and the plains of Troy, an account of which, written, it would seem, about 1868, he has given in the first volume of his recent work. This volume contains, *inter alia*, the result of his studies among the "Cyclopean" works in Argolis, a knowledge of great value to him when he commenced his more important excavations. He seems also, about this period, to have carefully examined the Troad, and to have satisfied himself that Hissarlik was the place at which to commence his excavations. Having married a Greek lady, in every sense a "help-meet" for the work he had set himself to do, he went again to the Troad in the spring of 1870, and, having secured an ample number of labourers, continued his excavations there during the greater part of the period between the autumn of 1871 and the summer of 1873.

It must not be supposed that this work was one of ease or pleasant toil: he had not the patient "Chaldeans" who did Layard's behests, still less had he

Hormuzd Rassam to settle, as a native only can settle, the ever-rising disputes between the Greek and Mussulman "navvies." Indeed, to secure one pavement from destruction, he had to tell his workmen that by this road "Christ had gone up to visit King Priam"! The cost, too, was very heavy; for he had often 150 men in his employment, and expended, from his own resources, fully £8,000. Is it possible to estimate too highly such exertions towards the ascertainment of the reality or falsity of ancient story, and this, too, by the only thoroughly effectual means, the excavation of sites of traditional importance? Can we withhold our admiration for the labourer, even though his enthusiasm may have led him to believe all he found was Trojan, the golden relics, especially, being those of King Priam? and, after all, what matters the theory of the excavator, so the work he does is well done? As well might we quarrel with Mr. Parker's labours in Rome, because he has coupled with his most valuable excavations his own, somewhat fanciful, belief in the personality of a Romulus. Every honest excavation, such as those of Dr. Schliemann and Mr. Parker, are so many landmarks recovered from all-destroying time. We can well afford to dispense with or to smile at the fancies of the excavators, so only that a careful record be kept of what the excavations have really revealed.

Dr. Schliemann's account of his diggings, between the autumn of 1871 and June 17, 1873, has been published in the form of twenty-three letters or memoirs; a mode of narrative the more pleasant that it places the reader *au courant* with the daily ideas of the discoverer, though, necessarily, causing some repetition and not a few corrections. His Introduction, however, gives a sufficient summary of what he accomplished. With the text he has also provided an atlas of 217 photographic plates of the plans and excavations carried on throughout the whole plain of Troy, together with representations of between three and four thousand individual objects discovered. These photographs—not, we regret to say, from the originals, but from drawings of them—are wholly inadequate to give any satisfactory idea of the beauty or character of the objects themselves.

Dr. Schliemann having, as we have stated, made up his mind[11] that the rising ground now called *Hissarlik* (or fortress) was the site of Old Troy, commenced his diggings there, on a plateau about 80 feet above the level of the plain, with a steep descent to the N.E. and N.W. Above this plateau is a portion of ground 26 feet higher, about 925 feet long by 620 feet wide, which he assumed to be the Pergamum of Homer, or citadel of Priam. If so, beneath and around this Acropolis must have been the second as well as the earlier city. Dr. Schliemann went to work much as miners do when they are "prospecting," only on a larger scale: he took soundings of the plain till he reached the virgin rock, at a depth never greater than 16 feet, at first meeting only with walls of houses and fragments of pottery of a Greek or even later period. As he found nothing else up to the edge of the Pergamum,[12] he concluded that the original Ilium did not spread into the plain, and that its area was accurately defined by the great wall he afterwards found. In short, he concluded that the city had no special Acropolis,[12] as feigned by Homer, and that any enlargement of the old town was due to the *débris* gradually thrown down or accumulated around the base of the small central hill. He adds, rather amusingly, "I venture to hope that the civilized world will not only not be vexed that the town of Priam has shown itself scarcely the twentieth part as large as was to be expected from the statements of the Iliad, but, on the contrary, that, with delight and enthusiasm, it will accept the certainty that Ilium did really exist."

<u>11</u>. Dr. Schliemann has fully stated in the *Augsburg Gazette*, Sept. 26, 1873, his reasons for accepting Hissarlik for Troy, and for rejecting Bounarbashi and other sites; and his reasons, to *an antiquary*, are weighty:—1. At Bounarbashi, nothing has been found earlier than potsherds of the sixth century B.C. 2. Sir J. Lubbock, in the so-called tomb of Hector, found nothing earlier than the third century B.C. 3. Von Hahn found neither potsherds nor bricks on the north side of the Balidagh, between the Akropolis (of Gergi) and the springs of Bounarbashi. 4. The sites examined by Clarke and Barker Webb, and that of Ulrichs, presented no remains of man. 5. The "village of the Ilians"—κώμη Ἰλιέων of Demetrius of Skepsis—gave forth nothing earlier than potsherds of the first century B.C. On the other hand, under Hissarlik, have been found all or most of the remains, treasure included, which Dr. Schliemann has secured.

<u>12</u>. This word Pergamum or Pergama, which occurs more than once in Asia Minor, notably in the case of the great city of that name, is probably only another form of the πύργος, *burg* or *berg*, which runs through so many languages of the Indo-European family. Thus, Sanskr. *spurg*; Gr. πυργ, originally σφυργος or φυργος. So the Gothic *bairg-ahei*, mountainous; *fairg-uni*, mountain. Compare, also, with this, Berge in Thrace, and Perge in Pamphylia. Possibly, the Celtic *briga* (*Brigantes*, the dwellers in the hills) is connected with the same root. The Arabs have now adopted the word (see Rénan).

There is nothing specially remarkable in the small size of the "supposed" Troy. It was an ancient custom to build the town round a central Acropolis where possible. So was it with Athens and Mycenæ, with Rome, Carthage and Mount Zion; the ordinary dwellings of the population for centuries being huts or small cottages, like the traditional *Tugurium* of Romulus, buildings which would, naturally, leave behind them no traces of their former existence. It has been well remarked, that Homer cannot fairly be accused of having *invented* this Pergamum, as the hill was a natural fact: and that what he really did, was, to indulge his imagination as to the magnificence of the town he grouped on it or in the plain round it.

The little hill of Hissarlik became, therefore, the centre of Dr. Schliemann's labours, the most productive field of his excavations, and the site where he laid open walls far more ancient than Greek Ilium, with a perfect entrance-gateway and paved road through it, together with many remains of houses, and a marvellous collection of relics, some of great intrinsic value. But the most unexpected discovery was the *position* of the various remains, proving, as this did, that, at least, four different sets of people had occupied this site, and covered it with their own buildings, in complete unconsciousness that there had been elder races there before them, whose remains were actually under them. The same fact has been noticed, but on a small scale, elsewhere. Thus Roman London lies some sixteen or seventeen feet under the Mansion House or Bank of England; so, too, Layard found successive traces on the mound of Nimrud of Arab, Roman, and Parthian occupation. But such traces are as nothing to what Dr. Schliemann's works revealed. It was clear that the natural hill of Hissarlik had been, at first, somewhat levelled, being also, in some places, made more secure by a retaining wall, and that, above this, the successive ruins have been heaped up in a solid mass from 46 to 52 feet above the native rock. On this, lastly, *Novum Ilium* was built. Dr. Schliemann gives a section, whence it appears that, commencing from the existing surface, Greek Ilium occupies about six feet in depth; that at 23 feet below this, Dr. Schliemann's "Troy of Homer" is reached; and that, under this "Troy," again, is a third stratum 29 feet thick, the whole human accumulations. The most sceptical person on the subject of "Troy divine" cannot question the accuracy of Dr. Schliemann's measurements, whatever he may think of his theories. It is manifest that even the stratum immediately under Ilium Novum is essentially prehistoric. Of what date, then, are the still lower strata? Indeed, calculations, on such a point, can as little be relied on as those of Mr. Horner on the *alluvium* of the Egyptian Delta. There are, however, some matters connected with them that must be noticed from their peculiarity. Thus the super-imposed layers testify to periods of occupation rather than to those of destruction; while the theory of distinct and well-defined stone, bronze, and iron ages completely breaks down, stone implements occurring in all the strata, and even where bronze is abundant. Iron, on the other hand, is almost wholly absent. Thus instruments of stone and of copper occur with ornaments in gold, silver, and even ivory, evidencing, as these do, advance in civilization and, as the cause of this, some interchange of commerce with other nations.

Whatever else, therefore, may be thought of Dr. Schliemann's researches, it cannot be doubted but that the excavations at Hissarlik form a new chapter in the history of man, and as such [apart from any supposed connection with

Homer], are a sufficient reward for his labour and expenditure of capital. It would unquestionably have been better (but who shall control honest enthusiasm?) had he been less ready to invest every discovery he made with some Homeric name; we could have been well free of such pretentious identifications as the Tower of Ilium, the Scæan gates, the Royal Palace, and King Priam's Treasure; just as, in a similar case, Mr. Parker's valuable contributions to the early history of Rome are not improved by the revival of the legend of a Romulus and Remus, and of the suckling of these heroes by a she-wolf. Nothing, however, allowing for these slight blemishes, can exceed the interest of Dr. Schliemann's narrative.

"The excavations," to quote his own words, "prove that the second nation which built a town on this hill, upon the *débris* of the first settlers (which is from twenty to thirty feet thick), are the Trojans of whom Homer sings.... The strata of this Trojan *débris*, which, without exception, bears marks of great heat, consists mainly of red ashes of wood, and rise from five to ten feet above the great wall of Ilion, the double Scæan gate, and the great surrounding wall, the construction of which Homer ascribes to Poseidon and Apollo, and they show that the town was destroyed by a fearful conflagration. How great this heat must have been is clear also from the large slabs of stone of the road leading from the double Scæan gate down to the plain; for when a few months ago I laid this road open, all the slabs appeared as much uninjured as if they had been put down quite recently; but after they had been exposed to the air for a few days the slabs of the upper part of the road, to the extent of some 10 feet, which had been exposed to the heat, began to crumble away, and have now almost disappeared, while those of the lower portion of the road, which had not been touched by the fire, have remained uninjured, and seem to be indestructible. A further proof of the terrible catastrophe is furnished by a stratum of scoriæ of melted lead and copper of a thickness of from $\frac{1}{5}$ of an inch to $1\frac{1}{5}$ inch, which extends nearly through the whole hill at a depth of from 27 feet to 29 feet."

It was here that Dr. Schliemann found the prodigious structure he has named the "Tower of Ilion," a building no less than 40 feet thick. "This tower," he adds, "after having been buried for thirty-one centuries, and after, during thousands of years, one nation after another had built its houses and palaces high above its summit, has now again been brought to light, and commands a view, if not of the whole plain, at least of its northern parts, and of the Hellespont." A little way beyond this tower is a remarkably perfect gateway, fitted for two pairs of gates, one behind the other, the upper fastenings of which still remain in the stone posts. These Dr. Schliemann takes for the "Scæan gates" of Homer. He then came to what he calls the "Palace of Priam," no doubt, a house of some kind, at a depth of from 22 to 26 feet, resting upon the great tower, and directly under the Temple of Minerva. Its walls were built of small stones cemented with earth, and would seem to belong to different epochs. The walls vary in thickness from 4 feet to 1 foot 10 inches. All about, within as well as without, are abundant signs of fire, which must have burnt with prodigious fury. Dr. Schliemann speaks of many feet in thickness of red and yellow wood ashes. Here, as at Nineveh and at Carthage, the first destruction seems to have been fire, the great extent of it, in each case, having probably arisen from the wooden construction of the upper portions of these houses. At Nineveh, it has been reasonably supposed that only the foundations of the walls were of stone or brick, the upper part, like many Eastern houses at the present day, being wholly of wood, which would readily catch fire, and fill the rooms below with burning embers. In several of the rooms of one of these houses Dr. Schliemann found red jars from 7 to 8 feet high, and, to the east of the house, what he assumes to have been a sacrificial altar, a slab of granite 5 feet 4 inches long by 5 feet 5 inches broad. Such a conflagration, it is likely, would be long remembered; and it has been acutely asked whether, after all, there may not have been an Asiatic Iliad handed down from mouth to mouth, of which Homer may have availed himself, as did the mediæval Minnesingers.

The next and the greatest of Schliemann's discoveries was also one of his last: we give it in his own words. "In the course of excavations on the Trojan wall, and in the immediate neighbourhood of Priam's house, I lighted on a great copper object of remarkable form, which attracted my attention all the more, as I thought I saw gold behind. Upon this copper object rested a thick crust of red ashes and calcined ruins, on which again weighed a wall nearly 6 feet thick and 18 feet high, built of great stones and earth, and which must have belonged to the period next after the destruction of Troy. In order to save this treasure from the greed of my workmen, and to secure it for science, it was necessary to use the very greatest haste, and so, though it was not yet breakfast-time, I had "paidos," or resting-time, called out at once. While my workmen were eating and resting I cut out the treasure with a great knife, not without the greatest effort and the most terrible risk of my life, for the great wall of the fortress which I had to undermine, threatened every moment to fall upon me. But the sight of so many objects, of which each alone is of inestimable worth to science, made me foolhardy, and I thought of no danger. The carrying off, however, of the treasures would have been impossible without the help of my dear wife, who stood by ready to pack up the objects in her shawl as I cut them out, and to take them away."

We may add that the whole find lay together in a quadrangular mass, retaining the shape of the box in which it had been deposited, and that hard by was a large key, presumably that which once locked it. The treasure had, probably, been hastily packed, an idea fully sustained by its miscellaneous character. Indeed, the same thing seems to have happened in the case of the bronze plates found by Mr. Layard at Nineveh. The mass of precious metal found is simply astonishing, one cup alone weighing 40 oz. of gold, while there were besides, innumerable objects in bronze, silver and gold, spears and axes, and two-edged daggers, together with a large bronze shield, with a central boss, and a rim raised as if to receive the edges of ox-hides or other covering. Fortunately, the gold vessels had resisted the action of the fire; some of them having been cast, others hammered; in some cases, too, soldering had been used. One curious portion of the collection Dr. Schliemann describes as follows:—"That this treasure was packed," says he, "in the greatest haste, is shown by the contents of the great silver vase, in which I found, quite at the bottom, two splendid golden diadems, a fillet for the head, and four most gorgeous and artistic pendants for ear-rings. On them lay fifty-six golden ear-rings and 4,750 little golden rings, perforated prisms and dice, together with golden buttons and other precious things which belonged to other ornaments. After these, came six golden bracelets, and, quite at the top of all, in the silver vase, were two small golden cups."

Besides these more precious objects, Dr. Schliemann met with a quantity of what, for want of a better name, may be called idols, consisting of flat pieces of stone, marbles, and terra-cotta, [and, in one instance, of the vertebra of some antediluvian animal,] containing on one side "an attempt to model a face whether human or owlish." Such objects are not rare. In the British Museum are many flat pieces of burnt clay, with moulding on them, of the rudest kind, not wholly unlike what Dr. Schliemann found. Dr. Schliemann sees in these the original type of the sacred owl of Minerva,—to say the least,—a very bold guess. Indeed, but for the place where they were found, their remote antiquity might be doubted, as they might be, after all, but degraded types of a good period of art. Dr. Schliemann, however, maintains that many of these strange owl-headed objects of clay are representatives of Athene,—in fact, the original type of the γλαυκῶπις θεά, the "goddess with the bright or flashing eyes," and, also, that this epithet ought to be now translated the "owl-faced goddess"! But though Dr. Schliemann may urge in favour of his views that, as the worship of Athene was of Oriental origin, there is no reason why she should not have been represented as owl-faced, just as we find an eagle-headed Nisroch, a hawk-headed Ra, and a ram-headed Ammon, there is, really, no evidence in favour of his theory. Mr. Newton has embraced everything in his remark that "the conception of the human form as an organic whole, a conception we meet with in the very dawn of Greek art, nowhere appears" in Dr. Schliemann's collections, the probability being that these objects are of an antiquity long antecedent to anything Greek, and the work of a people in no way connected with the Greeks. In Greek art, the usual adjunct to most representations of Athene on coins is the owl, while in Homer (Odyss. iii. 372) Athene leaves Nestor, under the form of an osprey. It is possible, therefore, that these metamorphoses symbolize a still earlier faith.

Having already stated our belief that not only did an Ilium or a Troy really exist, but, also, that there was a real living Homer, we need not notice the objections urged against the opinions of Dr. Schliemann, on the ground that "as the Iliad is a mythical poem, it is absurd to expect in it any historical kernel," a method of reasoning, to say the least, unsatisfactory, if not fallacious. There is no conceivable reason why the most mythical poem may not comprehend contorted images of real events; the difficulty, in each case, and the only real difficulty, being the unravelling of the confused stories, which prevent our taking up the tangled skein of history. No one supposes the early legends of the Zendavesta to be history, yet some of the stations of the migration from N.E. to S.W. can be reasonably identified: so, too, no one supposes the story of Gyges in Herodotus historical, though the annals of Assur-bani-pal prove the reality of a "Gugu, king of Ludim." The prehistoric theory may be pressed too far.

Of the character of the art of the objects of Dr. Schliemann, or of the date of his wonderful collections, there is, at present, no evidence on which to base a reasonable judgment. One thing, however, seems certain; that they are not Greek—nor in any way connected with Greek art. If among the vast numbers of objects found, there may be some objects resembling others met with in Greece, the natural inference would be that, as so much of Greek art is traceable ultimately to Asia, so, too, are these. Nor must we, altogether, ignore the possible effects of commerce. Dr. Schliemann has certainly proved the existence of a wealthy population—living on the spot that tradition and history alike have assigned to Troy; and we cannot doubt that the owners of these remains were pre-Hellenic. It is not so long ago that Semiramis was as mythical a name as King Priam; and who can say that a future Rawlinson may not prove the truth of a Trojan Priam as clearly as that "Sammuramit" reigned in Nineveh? The dwellers on the rock of Ilion clearly were "no prehistoric savages," but denizens of a real city, with its fortress and palace. It is curious that, above Dr. Schliemann's "Trojans," at a distance of from 23 to 33 feet, dwelt a population who constructed their houses of small stones and earth, and, occasionally, of sun-dried bricks. The artistic remains of this people are inferior to those below them; yet they made coarse pottery, battle-axes, knives, nails, &c., with a slight use of copper or bronze, but with plenty of stone implements. This place, having been destroyed in its turn, another set of people occupied the mound, a race inferior in civilization to all who had preceded them. These people, it has been suspected, were Cimmerians, perhaps, portions of the Nomad tribes, who, we know from Herodotus and Strabo, constantly made eruptions into Asia Minor.

We must add that, among the various objects found by Dr. Schliemann, were some scratches of the rudest kind, on a honestone, from the first supposed to be letters of some alphabet. The truth of this conjecture has been recently proved by the persevering study of Professor Gomperz, of Vienna, who says that, in the comparisons he has made between the Cypriote alphabet and the Hissarlik inscriptions, "I have not schematized, I have not enlarged or reduced anything. Every dot, every twist is copied with slavish accuracy from the best Cyprian documents. Nor have I allowed myself to be eclectic and to mix letters of different periods and localities." Professor Max Müller adds, "Accepting these statements of Professor Gomperz, I can only repeat my conviction, that his decipherment of the first inscription *Tagoi Dioi* seems to me almost beyond reasonable doubt." The interpretation of the other presumed inscriptions is more open to doubt.

It is a remarkable fact, as clearly shown by Dr. Schliemann's researches, that the occupiers of all these strata, alike, were tillers of the ground, while the huge jars found standing upright can hardly have been used for any other purpose than the storing of wine, oil, or corn. The quantity of copper found suggests a connection with Cyprus—the island of copper—as do, also, the inscriptions just noticed; subsequent analysis, however, has thrown doubt on Dr. Schliemann's idea that his vessels were of pure copper.[13] The fine red pottery, too, is said to resemble very much the existing pottery of Cyprus. The vases are, however, not painted, nor have any traces of sculpture been as yet detected.

> 13. The Romans called their copper from Cyprus, *Cyprium*: but the name of the island is, more likely, from the Hebrew *Chopher*, the cypress tree.

In concluding these notes on Dr. Schliemann's collection, which, from our limited space, have been more condensed than we could have wished, we need only add that, besides the greater and richer monuments, Dr. Schliemann has found thousands of terra-cotta disks or wheels, each with a hole in the middle, the purport of which has considerably exercised the imaginations of the learned. Thus they have been called spindles, weights for sinking nets or weaving and *ex voto* tablets by Dr. Schliemann himself, &c. The variety of patterns on them is so great that, if anything but meaningless ornaments, it is impossible to suppose them all for one and the same purpose; and the patterns on some of them are unquestionably very curious. Thus we have scratches much resembling the earliest Chinese sacred characters; others, clearly astronomical; and, above all, that commonest of Buddhist symbols, the *Swastika*, a cross with arms curved or straight, and bent at right angles.

With regard to ILIUM NOVUM, or Hissarlik, which, as we have said, we believe occupies the site of the older city, we must say, that whatever doubts may have existed as to this point previously to Dr. Schliemann's excavations ought now to cease, as the Greek remains he has found there are unquestionably sufficient for this identification. How early Novum Ilium was founded cannot now be determined; but, as the place was one of some strength, it is reasonable to suppose it may have been occupied very soon after the fall of Old Troy, supposing, what, however, is not necessary, that Troy was wholly destroyed. When Xerxes passed, it was a place of importance, and the son of Xerxes recognized it as a Greek city. Alexander, too, like Xerxes, sacrificed there, and bestowed many favours on the population, notably as occupants of the presumed site of the ancient city; the Romans did the same, perhaps with the additional idea of protecting the traditional site whence they claimed their own descent (Liv. xxxvii. 37, xxxviii. 39). Sylla and Lucullus were, alike, friendly to it and Lucan asserts that, after Pharsalia, Julius Cæsar (mindful of his presumed ancestor Iulus) examined for himself these localities (cf. App. Bell. Mithr. c. 53; Plut. Vit. Syll.; Strab. xiii. 594; Lucan, ix. 967), at the same time instituting the "Ludi Trojani," noticed by Virgil and other writers (Æn. v. 602; Suet. Cæs. 39; Dio Cass. xliii. 23).[14]

> 14. The famous *Sigean* inscription (now in the British Museum), was procured by Lord Elgin from the porch of the village church on the promontory of Sigeum, a little way S. of Hissarlik. For many years it was supposed to be the oldest of Greek inscriptions; but it is probably not so old as some of those from Branchidæ procured by Mr. Newton, or, as the Greek inscription on the Colossus of Psammetichus at Abu-Simbel, in Nubia. Its object was to record the presentation of certain vessels for the use of the Prytaneium at Sigeum by Phanodicus and Hermocrates, a native of Proconnesus.

ALEXANDRIA TROAS (in the Acts of the Apostles simply Troas) has nothing really to do with the Trojan legend, but was an important place of commerce in Roman times, and the capital of the surrounding district. It was originally founded by Antigonus,[15] and is chiefly memorable for the remarkable munificence of a private individual, Herodes Atticus, who built an immense aqueduct, some traces of which still remain. Suetonius asserts that Julius Cæsar once thought of transferring Alexandria in Egypt to this place, and Zosimus adds that Constantine had, also, at one time designed it as the capital of his Eastern Empire (Suet. Cæs. c. 79; Zosimus, ii. 30); an idea, perhaps, preserved in its present name *Eski Stamboul.* It was thence that St. Paul and St. Luke set sail for Macedonia (Acts xvi. 11), and here, somewhat later, the Apostle restored the boy Eutychus to life (Acts xx. 9). Lastly, on rounding Cape Lectum, we come upon a deep and beautiful gulf, where stood the ancient town of *Adramyttium*, according to Strabo, a colony of the Athenians (xiii. 6), but, more probably, the creation of Adramys, the brother of Crœsus. It was early a place of considerable commerce, for which its admirable position well fitted it (Herod. vii. 42). Subsequently it was given by the Romans to the kings of Pergamus, but was almost obliterated by Mithradates (Strabo, xiii. p. 614). It was in a ship of Adramyttium that St. Paul commenced his voyage from Cæsarea to Italy to plead his cause before Nero (Acts xxvii. 2).

>15. The earliest coins of Alexandria Troas bear the name of Antigonia (Sestini. Mon. Vet. p. 76).

We come now to a city, PERGAMUM or PERGAMUS (for the name is used indifferently, though the latter or masculine form is, perhaps, the most common), which, regard being had to the fact, that, as a great town, it was not of remote antiquity, became in later days one of the most celebrated places of antiquity. It is said to have been a colony of the Heraclidæ from Arcadia (Pausan. i. 4, 5), and to have been first mentioned as a distinct city by Xenophon (Anab. vii. 8, 4), grouped, in all probability, round a fortress of considerable natural strength, whence, indeed, it derived its name. The commencement of its greatness was its selection by Lysimachus as his treasure city. Lysimachus was succeeded by Philetærus, and subsequently by Eumenes, Attalus Philetærus II. &c., a family remarkable for its noble deeds, as well as for the proverbial wealth of many of its members. Thus Attalus I., who was proclaimed King of Pergamus for his glorious victory over the Gaulish invaders, was eminent alike for his military skill, and for his political foresight (Polyb. xviii. 29; Liv. xxxiii. 21) in espousing the cause of the Romans. Eumenes II., no less than his father, the firm friend of the Romans, is worthy of record for the great library he formed at his capital city, held in antiquity to be second only to that of Alexandria (Strab. xiii. p. 264; Athen. i. 3).[16] It is said that in this library skins were first used for writing on, and that, from the title given to these sheets—"Pergamenæ chartæ"—we derive the name of "Parchment" (Varr. ap. Plin. xiii. 11).[17] The last of the Attali, after a reign of five years, dying childless, left his kingdom by his will to the Romans (Strab. xiii. 624, xiv. 646). Mr. Arundell gives a picturesque account of his ascent to the citadel, and of the magnificent view thence.

>16. This library was given by Antony to Cleopatra.

>17. Περγαμηνή χάρτη, or parchment, appears to have been brought into use by Crates of Mallos when Ptolemy cut off the supply of the *byblus* or the *papyrus* reed.

Immediately following on *Mysia* to the S. is the great province of *Lydia*, the portion of it fronting the Ægean bearing generally the name of *Ionia*, with a small district at its N.W. corner, touching Mysia, named *Æolis*. It was a popular belief that the Æolians were the first great body of Greek colonists to settle in Asia Minor, but, curiously, the name of Æolians does not occur in Homer. Strabo makes their advent to Asia Minor four generations earlier than the Ionian migration, and this movement has been supposed to have been contemporary with the return of the Heracleidæ, and may, not improbably, have been, in some degree, caused by it. In common with the other Greek colonies, the Æolians became subject to Crœsus, and, on the success of Cyrus, were annexed to the Persian empire; hence, in the Græco-Persian war, they contributed sixty ships to the armament of Xerxes. The principal towns of Æolis were Myrina, Cyme, Neontichos, and Methymna. They are not, however, of sufficient importance to detain us here. Pass we, therefore, to *Ionia*.

CHAPTER II.

Phocæa—Smyrna—Clazomenæ—Erythræ—Teos—Colophon—Ephesus—Mr. Wood—Miletus—Branchidæ or Didyma—Sacred Way—Mr. Newton—Thyateira—Magnesia ad Sipylum—Philadelphia—Tralles—Sardes—Halicarnassus—Mausoleum—Cnidus—Demeter—Lion-Tomb—Mr. Pullan—Physcus—Caunus—Stratonicea—Aphrodisias—Mylasa and Labranda.

PHOCÆA—the most northern of the Ionian cities—founded by emigrants from *Phocis*, under two Athenian chiefs, soon, from the excellence of its harbour, secured a prominent place among the early maritime states of the world, and was the first to establish colonies on the Adriatic, the coasts of Etruria, Gaul, and Spain. It is reported that Arganthonius, then king of Tartessus (probably Tarshish), did all he could to persuade these enterprising strangers to stay in his land; and that, failing this, he gave them large sums of money to build (or rebuild) the walls of their native town. Phocæa is often mentioned subsequently, though it does not appear to have performed any very memorable actions. It may be traced by its coins, and by the annalists and ecclesiastical writers to the latest period of the Byzantine empire. Indeed, so late as A.D. 1421, the Genoese built a new town near its ancient site, which still retains the name of *Palaio-Phoggia*.

A little further to the S. we come to SMYRNA, one of the most celebrated cities of Asia Minor, though it was comparatively late in attaining this eminence. It was situated on a bay of unrivalled beauty and commercial excellence; and, almost alone of the great cities or ports of Western Asia has preserved its eminence to the present day, being now, as it has long been, the chief emporium of the Levant trade. In remote times, Smyrna successfully resisted the attacks of Gyges, king of Lydia, and was, in consequence, taken and destroyed by his successor, Alyattes. It is said, that, after this blow, it was nearly deserted for 400 years, but was, at length, rebuilt by Antigonus and Lysimachus, though not exactly on the same site. With this rebuilding its great prosperity commenced. Nor were the claims to distinction advanced by itself inferior to its real greatness. Inscriptions abound (some of the best, indeed, among the marbles at Oxford), where, as on its coins, it calls itself ΠΡΩTH ACIAC, the "first city of Asia"; and so, indeed, it long continued, though at times suffering severely from civil wars and earthquakes, and most of all from the merciless treatment of Tímúr. Smyrna claimed, especially, to be the birthplace of Homer, and dedicated a temple to him. A cave was also shown there, in which the poet was said to have composed his verses (Pausan. Ach. 5). Smyrna is not, however, mentioned by Homer. In the reign of Tiberius, Smyrna contended with ten other cities for the honour (?) of erecting a temple to that worthless ruler, and won the prize; and here, not many years later, the Christian Church flourished under Polycarp, its first bishop, who is believed to have suffered martyrdom in its stadium about A.D. 166.

Next to Smyrna we may take CLAZOMENÆ, a town whose date is probably not earlier than the Ionic migration. It was famous as the birthplace of Anaxagoras, the philosopher, whose disciple Archelaus taught Socrates and Euripides; and, also, as one of the states which joined with the Phocæans in founding the naval colony of Naucratis in Egypt (Herod. ii. 178). It retained its name and existence till late in the Byzantine period (Plin. v. 31; Ptol.; Hierocl. Synecd.), but, towards the middle of the eleventh century, was finally destroyed by the Turks.

ERYTHRÆ, celebrated as the home of one if not of two Sibyls—and a town whose life is traceable by coins and inscriptions to a late period of the Roman empire, and, from the acts of Councils and other ecclesiastical documents, was manifestly for some time an episcopal see. Its land produced good wine [being called in a distich preserved by Athenæus φερεστάφυλος Ἐρύθρα (Erythra yielding bunches of grapes)],[18] and fine wheaten flour:—TEOS (now Sighajik), the birthplace of Anacreon and of Hecatæus the historian; famous, too, for its temple, dedicated to Bacchus, some remains of which have been published by the Society of Dilettanti, and, recently, more fully examined by Mr. Pullan:—COLOPHON, an early Ionian settlement, once the possessor of a flourishing navy, and of cavalry reputed victorious wherever employed;[19] and illustrious for its poets, Mimnermus, Phœnix, and Hermesianax, and, possibly even Homer; till at length it was destroyed by Lysimachus:—PRIENE, the birthplace of the philosopher and statesman Bias, and still identifiable by considerable ruins near the Turkish village of Samsoun, to the S. of Mycale, with a famous Temple of Minerva Polias, the ruins of which have been engraved in the "Ionian Antiquities." In Chandler's time, about 100 years ago, the whole circuit of the city walls was still standing.

18. The lines are—

ἐν δὲ φερεσταφύλοις Ἐρυθραῖς ἐκ κλιβάνου ἐλθὼν

λευκὸς ἁβραῖς θάλλων ὥραις τέρψει παρὰ δεῖπνον.

Archestr. ap. Athen. iii. 112, B.

19. From this continued success arose the proverb, τὸν Κολοφῶνα ἐπέθηκεν "he has brought the work to a completion." And, hence, the final letters or signature at the end of a book have been termed the *colophon*.

But of the cities of W. Asia, no one took a higher place than EPHESUS; though not one of the most ancient, or noticed by Homer. Pliny ascribes its origin to the Amazons; and Strabo gives an excellent account of its site, the chief feature of which was a celebrated port called Panormus, with the temple of Diana, one of the Seven Wonders of the world, at a little distance without the city walls. The worship of this Diana (of Asiatic origin, and symbolized by her peculiar statue) was earlier than the planting of the Ionian colony by Androcles, as has been reasonably suspected, on a hill called Coressus, the lower ground (ultimately the chief part of the city) having been only gradually built over. After its first colonization we hear nothing of Ephesus till the time of Crœsus, who is said to have failed to take the town, owing to a device of a certain Pindarus, who attached the city to the temple by a rope, thus making the intervening space sacred, or an asylum. On this the story goes, that Crœsus, of all princes then ruling, a lover of the gods, spared, indeed, the city, but showed his common sense by changing its constitution and banishing Pindarus. It further appears that Crœsus dedicated golden bulls at Ephesus, and helped largely in the construction of the first temple dedicated there. The temple we now know was about 1,400 yards from the city, a fact, apparently, not anticipated by the first modern investigators of its site.

The inhabitants of Ephesus, as a rule, were time-servers, and ready to court the support of whosoever for the time being were their most powerful neighbours. Thus, at first, they joined the Ionian revolt; then, on the overthrow of Xerxes, were for a while tributary to Athens; and then, again, after the victories of Lysander, permitted their city to be the head-quarters of the Spartan operations against Asia Minor; though he could not, however, persuade the people to change the name of their city to that of his wife Arsinoe. After the overthrow of Antiochus, Ephesus was added by the Romans to the kingdom of Pergamus.

Again, when Mithradates was all-powerful, we find the people of Ephesus, to please him, joining in a general massacre of the Romans in their town; indeed, going to such lengths as not to respect the asylum of their own temple; the natural result being a severe punishment of this fickle population on the ultimate success of the Romans. On an inscription, however, recently discovered, we believe, by Mr. Wood, but now at Oxford, the people assert that they had been compelled to act against their will, and that they were none the less, at heart, the devoted friends of the Romans. As a place of commercial importance, Ephesus did not survive the first three centuries of the Roman empire, as the city was sacked by the Goths in A.D. 262, and its famous temple burnt, an event of which some traces have been detected during the recent excavations on its site. In later days it passed into the hands of the Seljuks and Turks, and a great mosque was built there by Selim I. on the rising ground overlooking the port. The long occupation of the site of

Ephesus by a mixed population is attested by the discovery there by Mr. Wood of a hoard of coins, belonging chiefly to the Western States of Europe, and struck during the thirteenth and fourteenth centuries. Among these are some of the Christian subjects of Saro-khan, an emir of Magnesia in the fourteenth century.[20] It is believed that the present name of its site, Aiosoluk, is a corruption of Hagios Theologos (St. John), the name borne by Ephesus during the Middle Ages.

> 20. An interesting account of these coins (2,231 in number) has been given in the Numism. Chron., vol. xii. New Ser., 1872, by Mr. H. A. Grueber, of the British Museum. The whole "find," with some lumps of metal, weighed more than seventeen pounds of silver. Among these were coins of Naples, of Rhodes, of the Seljuk Amírs, of Venice, Genoa, and of the Papal States, their dates embracing a period of about eighty years, from A.D. 1285.

The chief glory of Ephesus was its temple. According to the most ancient reports, there had been in remote times one, at least, of the grandest proportions which Herodotus claims, with that of Juno at Samos, as among the greatest works of the Greeks. Its architect is said to have been contemporary with Theodorus and Rhœcus, the builders of the Samian Heræum, early in the sixth century B.C.; and Xenophon, especially, notices it, as he deposited there the share entrusted to him of the tenth, arising from sale of the slaves of the Ten Thousand at Cerasus, which was appropriated to Apollo and Artemis.[21] We have here an instance of a custom noticed elsewhere,—viz., that the great temples of the Hellenic world were often used as banks of deposit, where treasure was collected, not merely in the form of *anathemata* or dedicated objects, but, also, in large quantities of bullion, &c., *in trust*. Many inscriptions in Boeckh show clearly that the administrators of the temples employed these treasures as loans. Artemis was, in fact, a queen, whose dower was the wealth accumulated in her temple. As is well known, the original (or the second temple of Artemis, for this point is not clear) was burnt by Herostratus, in B.C. 356, traditionally, on the same night on which Alexander the Great was born, but it was soon rebuilt. It would take a whole book, says Pliny, to describe all its details, and it is admitted to have been the largest temple of antiquity.

> 21. In Pausanias, vii. 11, will be found a very full and interesting account of the worship of the Ephesian Artemis, but it is too long to quote here. Pindar says, the worship was instituted by the Amazons, Crêsos or Korêsos, an autochthon, and Ephesus, the son of the river god Cayster, being the first builders of the temple. For details of the older temples, see Strab. xiv. 641; Xen. Anab. v. 3; Plin. xvi. 79; and Vitruv. x. 6.

Among other valuables, the temple contained the famous picture by Apelles of Alexander, while the circuit round it was an asylum where debtors and worse rogues could screen themselves from justice, an evil which, as an inscription recently found there shows, Augustus found it needful to restrain within reasonable limits. Ephesus, too, was the usual port where the Roman proconsuls landed, on their way to their several provinces. Thus, Cicero came to Ephesus when going to his government in Cilicia. So, too, Metellus Scipio put in there before Pharsalia, and M. Antonius after Philippi. There, too, also, was collected the fleet of Antony and Cleopatra before the fatal day of Actium.[22]

> 22. Le Quien's "Oriens Christianus" gives a list of seventy Christian bishops of Ephesus from Timothy to A.D. 1721. A good many of the later ones could only have been bishops in name.

But the most interesting matter to us in connection with Ephesus have been Mr. Wood's excavations there, with his discovery not only of many unexpected monuments of the ancient town, but of undoubted relics of the famous temple itself. Mr. Wood, as the constructing engineer of the Smyrna and Aidin Railway, had naturally become well acquainted with the neighbourhood of Ephesus, and, hence, so early as 1863, had made, at his own expense, some excavations, clearing out thereby the Odeum, and ascertaining the true position of the Magnesian and Coressian gates. In these researches, he met with several valuable inscriptions, one of them referring to a certain Roman, Publius Vedius Antoninus, who was at the time the γραμματεὺς—the Scribe or Town-clerk—of the city.[23] By degrees the position of the Theatre, the scene of the tumult at the time of St. Paul's visit, was clearly made out; but where was the Temple? In the prosecution of his excavations Mr. Wood had, however, met with many decrees of the people of Ephesus relating to the Temple,—one of them containing much curious information about the ritual used in the Temple-worship, with lists of the votive offerings, to be carried on certain days in procession "through the Magnesian Gate to the Great Theatre, and thence back again through the Coressian Gate to the Temple." Among the list of statues are several of Diana, probably, such as those which "Demetrius and his craftsmen" manufactured in the days of St. Paul.

> 23. Colonel Leake, in 1824, seems to have given the first sensible suggestion as to where the temple ought to be sought for. The Admiralty chart of 1836 (the foundation of the maps of Kiepert 1841-1846) and of Guhl (1843), afforded also the first accurate survey of the Gulf of Scala Nova. In 1862, Mr. Falkener suggested the head of the harbour to the west of the city as the most likely site.

DRUM OF PILLAR.

At length, in April, 1869, Mr. Wood came upon some massive walls, which were proved to have been those of the courtyard in which the Temple had once stood, by an inscription in Greek and Latin, stating that Augustus had rebuilt them; and, finally, in 1870, a marble pavement was lighted on, at the depth of nineteen feet below the alluvial soil of the present plain, together with drums of columns, quite six feet high, one base being still attached to its plinth. The site of the Temple of Diana had been reached, and its style was, at once, seen to have been similar to that of the Temple of Athene Polias at Priene, and of Apollo at Branchidæ. It is scarcely possible to speak too highly of Mr. Wood's tact and sagacity. Thus, considering the accounts of ancient authors too vague as guides for excavation, his first diggings were essentially tentative, and with the view of meeting with some illustrative inscriptions. In the Great Theatre he was more likely to find them than anywhere else, and here, indeed, he discovered six large stones, originally from the cella of the Temple, and each bearing various decrees. Indeed, by the most important of these, to which we have already alluded, the real clue was afforded as to its whereabouts. The of finding this inscription confirmed Mr. Wood's original idea of feeling his way to the Temple from one of the city gates, the result being the discovery of two roads,—one of them leading round the mountain Prion or Pion, the other towards the town of Magnesia. He wisely determined to trace the one which showed the greatest amount of wear or use, assuming that if either of them led to the Temple it would be the most used one. In the one round Mount Prion he found four distinct ruts, deeply cut in its pavement of huge blocks of marble, while the other road was worn scarcely at all. He then devoted all his energy, to use his own words, "in exploring the road round Mount Pion,[24] which eventually led to the Temple."

> 24. The spelling of the name of this little eminence does not seem to be quite certain. Pausanias and Pliny call it Pion; Strabo, on the other hand, Prion. There was a mountain so named in the island of Cos. Comp. *Priene*.

In this way, the peribolus, or courtyard wall of the Temple, was soon reached, and, not long after, as before stated, the drums of several of the columns were exhumed, lying in a confused mass as they had fallen, sixteen or seventeen centuries ago. The largest and best preserved of these drums, of which a sketch is given as the frontispiece for this volume, was found on February 3rd, 1871; it is somewhat more than 6 feet high and 18½ feet in circumference, and weighs 11¼ tons. From the figures carved on it, one of which represents Mercury, it may be fairly presumed that it was one of the thirty-six "columnæ cælatæ" recorded by Pliny. Mr. Wood states that though this splendid building was not only destroyed by earthquakes and the malice of man, all the stones, moreover, having been carried away that could be used for building purposes, enough still remained to enable him to draw out on paper an accurate plan of its original shape and *contour*. He adds that, in the course of his excavations, he "discovered the remains of three distinct temples, the last but two, the last but one, and the last. The former must have been that built 500 B.C., for which the solid foundations described by Pliny and Vitruvius were laid.... Between 5 and 6 feet below the pavement and under the foundations of the walls of the cella, I found the layer of charcoal, 4 inches thick, described by Pliny. This was laid between two layers of a composition about 3 inches thick, similar to, and of the consistency of, glazier's putty."

In conclusion, we may add that Mr. Wood found abundant instances of the use of colour, chiefly vermilion and blue, and one specimen of gold inserted, as a fillet; together with several pieces of friezes much shattered, but, evidently, of the same size and artistic character as the reliefs on the drum. The reliefs themselves do not exhibit any great artistic merit, though they fairly represent the characteristic style of the Macedonian period: their general effect must, however, have been very rich and gorgeous, and quite in character with what we know of rich and luxurious Ephesus. We have not, at present, any evidence that the columns, as well as the drums, were covered with sculpture. Mr. Wood, we believe, thinks they were, but a medallion in the Bibliothèque at Paris, which gives the front of the Temple, rather suggests the contrary.

Passing on from Ephesus we come to the scarcely less celebrated city of MILETUS, the parent, according to Pliny, of more than 80 colonies.[25]

Situated at the mouth and, on the left bank, of the Mæander, Miletus more strictly belongs to Caria; but it was, also, one of the most conspicuous members of the Ionian confederacy. It is believed that it was originally founded by a colony from Crete, under the leadership of Sarpedon, the brother of Minos; an idea, in some degree, confirmed by a notice in Homer (Il. ii. 867). Herodotus (ix. 97) only mentions Sarpedon's establishing himself in Lycia. The advantageous position of the town, with a harbour capable of holding a large fleet, naturally gave it, from the earliest times, the lead in maritime affairs. Its most important colonies were Abydus, Lampsacus, and Parium on the Hellespont; Proconnesus and Cyzicus on the Propontis; Sinope and Amisus on the Euxine; with several more on the coast of Thrace and Tauris, and on the Borysthenes. The period, however, of Miletus's chief power was comprised between its Ionian colonization and its conquest by the Persians in 494 B.C. After that period, it did not maintain the same lead among the seaports of the Asiatic Greeks; indeed, during the time of its greatest fame, peace was practically unknown among its people, who were constantly distracted by factions aristocratic or democratic.

> 25. Rambach—De Mileto ejusque coloniis (Hal. Sax. 1790)—has attempted, not without success, to identify the larger number of them.

As was natural, the kings of Lydia made many attempts to possess themselves of Miletus. In the reign of Alyattes, however, the Lydian and Milesian quarrel was, for the time, made up, the Lydian king having been supposed to have incurred the wrath of the gods, as his troops had burnt a temple dedicated to Minerva at Assessos. Some of the rulers of the town were men of historic note, especially Thrasybulus, the friend of the Corinthian Periander. Somewhat later, the Milesians made a treaty with Crœsus, and, what was of more importance to them, secured its maintenance by Cyrus; hence, their town was spared much of the misery inflicted on the other Ionian states in the first war with the Persians (Herod. i. 141, 143). But if Miletus had been previously fortunate, this good luck deserted her during the great Græco-Persian war; nor could she indeed complain, as the chief promoter of this rebellion was her "tyrannus" Histiæus. As will be remembered, it was mainly through Histiæus and his kinsman Aristagoras, that Ionia revolted against the Persians; and, further, that, to the instigations of the latter, was due the needless burning of the great western capital of the Persians, Sardes. An immediate attack on Miletus by the Persian satraps was the natural reply to this treachery; and the city was eventually taken by storm, with all the horrors consequent thereon.[26] It may be doubted, whether after this fall, Miletus ever again recovered her former glory.

> 26. Herodotus, vi. 18-21, states that the Athenians were so much distressed at the fall of Miletus, that they fined the poet Phrynichus

1,000 drachmæ for putting on the stage a drama entitled "The Capture of Miletus."

Subsequently, Miletus made many spasmodic efforts to regain her freedom, but with little avail, though it still existed till the decline of the Byzantine empire—its Church being under the direction of bishops who ranked as Metropolitans of Caria (Hierocl.).[27] A pestilential swamp now covers the birthplace of Thales, Anaximander, and Anaximenes.[28]

> 27. At Miletus, St. Luke tells us that St. Paul sent to his chief disciples at Ephesus (distant about thirty miles) to come to see him. This was their last opportunity, as he was then on his final journey to Jerusalem (Acts xx. 17).
>
> 28. A proverb cited by Athenæus from Aristotle may refer to the condition of the Milesians after the capture of their city by the Persians:—Πάλαι ποτ' ἦσαν ἄλκιμοι Μιλήσιοι.

In the neighbourhood of Miletus stood, at BRANCHIDÆ or Didyma, the famous temple of Apollo Didymæus, the site, we feel pleased to say, of one of Mr. Newton's most valuable researches. It was known in Greek history from the remotest times, as the site of a shrine and of an oracle second only in sanctity and importance to that of Delphi; as the spot where Pharaoh Necho dedicated the armour he had worn when he took the city of Cadytis (Herod, ii. 159), and as a place which received from Crœsus, before his war with Cyrus, golden offerings equal in weight to those he gave to Delphi. It was plundered and burnt by Darius I., and, a second time, by Xerxes, its sacred family of priests having been, on this occasion, swept off to Sogdiana by the conqueror; but it revived again, in renewed splendour, towards the close of the Peloponnesian war, when rebuilt on a scale so vast that, according to Strabo, it could not be roofed over: it was memorable, especially, too, for a succession of oracles ascending to a period before the commencement of history, yet not wholly extinct even so late as the days of Julian. It was reasonable to expect that such a place would retain some relics of its past greatness, and of its pre-eminence among the sacred shrines of antiquity. Indeed, many travellers, before Mr. Newton, had spoken of the ruins of the Temple and of the Sacred Way leading to it, and, from the notices in Wheler (1685), Gell, Leake, the "Ionian Antiquities," and Hamilton, much valuable information may be gathered.

It was left to Mr. Newton to complete what had been indeed, hardly done at all before, and to secure for England the most important sculptures still *in situ*. The Temple of Apollo Didymæus[29] was originally approached from the sea by a "SACRED WAY," on each side of which had once been a row of seated statues, sepulchral *sori*, tombs, &c. Along this "Way" Mr. Newton discovered eight seated statues, generally about 4 feet 6 inches high, by 2 feet

9 inches broad and deep; the character of their workmanship being, at the first glance, strikingly Egyptian, at least in this respect, that their drapery, extending from the shoulders to the feet, consists of one closely-fitting garment (*chitōn*), and of a light shawl (*peplos*). One only of the figures retains its head, the sculptured treatment of it being that usually recognized as the most archaic Greek, in that the hair is arranged in long parallel tresses, as in the earliest coins of Syracuse. With two exceptions, all these statues belong to the same period of art. Mr. Newton says, it is evident that no one of them occupied, when he discovered them, exactly its original position, and that they must, at some time or other, have been thrown down and partially removed—an opinion confirmed by a somewhat later discovery of about eighty feet of the original paving of the "SACRED WAY," together with some bases, not improbably those on which these statues had been originally placed. The "SACRED WAY" can still be traced for about 580 yards.

> 29. Didyma was the ancient name of the site where the temple stood; hence the building was sometimes called the "Didymæum." Strabo speaks of it as τοῦ ἐν Διδύμοις ναοῦ. On the pretence that the priests of Branchidæ voluntarily returned with Xerxes to Persia, their descendants were cruelly murdered by Alexander the Great (Strabo, xiv. 634, xi. 517; Quint. Curt., vii. 5).

INSCRIPTION OF CHARES.

In a wall extending along it are, here and there, masses of polygonal masonry, with individual stones of immense size, the remains, probably, of an original Hellenic wall. At a short distance from the last of the seated statues, Mr. Newton met with two remarkable monuments—a colossal lion and a female sphinx—both, unfortunately, much injured. The sphinx was completely buried under the earth, and had nothing in its form to recommend it, but the lion had, on its side, a very ancient inscription, which the barbarous Greeks of the neighbourhood had done all they could to obliterate. The important question is, to what period are these works to be assigned? Now, of direct evidence we have none; for, though history speaks of the two temples at this spot, we have no record of the statues themselves; the probability being that they were damaged nearly as much as at present before Herodotus visited the spot, and, probably, by the Persians. Yet, in spite of the silence of history, we have some indirect evidence from the monuments themselves; enough, at least, to determine their age within tolerably accurate limits. In the first place, we have the character of their art, which is, unquestionably, very archaic; secondly, on three of the chairs are inscriptions in the oldest Greek character; on the most important one written *boustrophedon* (*i.e.* backwards and forwards, as an ox ploughs); thirdly, a long inscription on the recumbent lion, and another, quite as old, on a detached block, the base, possibly, of a statue now lost. In order that the nature of the characters used may be comprehended, we annex a woodcut of the legend on one of the chairs of the seated figures, the translation of which is, "I am Chares, son of Clesis, ruler of Teichaoessa, a [dedicatory] monument of Apollo."[30] On the block found near the chair, the inscription states that "the sons of Anaximander have [dedicated a statue?] of Andromachus," and that "Terpsicles made it": while that, on the side of the lion,—the most curious of them all,—declares that "the sons of Python, Archelaos, Thales, Pasikles, Hegesander, and Lysias, have dedicated the offerings, as a tenth, to Apollo." Some years since, a still more perfect seated figure was in existence, on the chair of which was an inscription copied by Sir W. Gell and Mr. Cockerell, and published by Boeckh and Rose.[31]

> 30. This inscription was probably attached to a portrait statue. Teichioessa, or Teichiousa, we know from Thucydides (viii. 26, 28), was a strong place near Miletus. Athenæus (viii. 351) spells it Teichiûs. Mr. Newton suggests that Chares was probably one of the petty rulers on the western coast of Asia Minor in the sixth and fifth centuries B.C., of whom Herodotus notices more than one. A *bon-mot* of Stratonicus the musician is recorded by Athenæus: "As Teichioessa was inhabited by a mixed population, he observed that most of the tombs were those of foreigners, on which he said to his lad, 'Let us be off, since strangers seem to die here, but not one of the natives'" (viii. p. 351). Teichoessa was also famous for the excellence of its mullets (Ital. *triglia*),
>
> ... χειμῶνι δὲ τρίγλην
>
> ἔσθι' ἐνὶ ψαφαρῇ ληφθεῖσαν Τειχιοέσσῃ
>
> Μιλήτου κώμῃ.—Archestr. ap. Athen. *l. c.*
>
> 31. Colonel Leake (Journal of a Tour in Asia Minor, Lond., 1824, p. 239) has given an account of this chair, and suggests that the arrangement of these statues is similar to that of the avenues of the temples in Egypt. In a note to p. 342 of Colonel Leake's work, is a brief memoir by the late C. J. Cockerell, in which he suggests that the temple at Branchidæ was never completed, as the flutings of the

columns are not finished (see, also, pp. 347, 348). There is an engraving of this chair in the "Ionian Antiquities."

CHAIR FROM BRANCHIDÆ.

We cannot discuss here the character of the inscriptions quoted above, but all palæographers admit that the writing belongs to the earliest Greek period, not improbably anterior to the year B.C. 520. It may be still earlier, as, on the lion inscription, we find the name of Hegesander and another name, which, though the first letter has met with an injury, we agree with Mr. Newton in thinking, must be read as Thales, while, on the detached block, we have that of Anaximander. Now it is certainly remarkable that on two adjoining stones, found close to the most sacred temple of the Milesians, the names of two of the most celebrated philosophers of that town should occur. If, then, these be really the names of those philosophers, they may be supposed to have joined with other citizens of Miletus in dedicating the figure of the lion, and of the object (whether statue or otherwise) once attached to the second inscription; and, if so, the dates of these works would be between B.C. 470 and B.C. 560. Anaximander was born about B.C. 610, and Hegesander was probably the father of Hecatæus, who was himself born about B.C. 520.

It is worthy of remark that, unlike so many other early Greek works, these sculptures exhibit no trace of an Asiatic or Assyrian origin. The only style they recall is that of Egypt, while the only Assyrian monument they resemble is the semi-Egyptian seated figure brought by Mr. Layard from Kalah Sherghat. Mr. Newton has justly pointed out that the resemblance to

Egyptian work "is seen not only in the great breadth of the shoulders, but also in the modelling of the limbs, in which the forms of the bones and muscles are indicated with far greater refinement and judgment than at first sight seems to be the case ... the subdued treatment of the anatomy contributes to the general breadth and repose for which these figures are so remarkable, and suggests the idea that they were executed by artists who had studied in Egypt." We know that the Greeks were intimately connected with Psammetichus I., Amasis, and Neco; while the tombs at Cameirus, in Rhodes, have yielded works almost certainly imitated from Egyptian prototypes by early Greek artists. We have, too, the statement of Diodorus, that Theodorus of Samos and his brother Telecles of Ephesus, the sons of Rhoecus, derived the canon of their sculptures from Egypt. The general character, however, of the ornamentation, the mæander-pattern, and the lotos and borders on the garments of the seated figures, agreeing, as these do, with the same patterns on early Greek vases, tend to show that their actual artists were Greeks. Thus, too, the archaic statue of Athene in the Acropolis at Athens is essentially Greek, and not Egyptian. Pliny has further noticed that two Cretan sculptors, Dipænos and Scyllis, were the first artists (about B.C. 580) of note, as workers in marble: it is, therefore, quite conceivable that they may have been the actual artists of these monuments.

We shall now say a few words of THYATEIRA, MAGNESIA AD SIPYLUM, PHILADELPHIA, and TRALLES with some rather fuller remarks on the celebrated city, SARDES, the capital of Lydia.

THYATEIRA was a place of considerable importance, and probably of early origin, but of no great rank among the surrounding towns till the time of the Macedonians; its best known name, according to Steph. Byzant., being due to Seleucus Nicator. To us, its chief interest is its connection with early Christianity, as the home of "Lydia the seller of purple" (Acts xvi. 14), and as one of the Seven Churches of the Apocalypse. There are still, according to Sir Charles Fellows, remains of a considerable city; and it is also, under the name of Ak-Hissar, a flourishing commercial town. Close to the Lake Gygæa, not far from Sardes, was the sepulchral mound of Alyattes, considered by Herodotus one of the wonders of Lydia. This remarkable tumulus, which is about 280 yards in diameter, has been recently excavated by M. Spiegenthal, who discovered in its centre a sepulchral chamber of highly polished marble blocks, and of about the same size as that of the tomb of Cyrus. Such tumuli are common in Asia Minor; indeed, round the same lake, are three or four more, probably, as Strabo has suggested, the tombs of other early Lydian kings. Sir Gardner Wilkinson has pointed out that their structure—a stone basement with a mound of earth above—resembles the constructed tombs of Etruria.

The *Lydian* MAGNESIA—usually called "*Ad Sipylum*," to distinguish it from the Magnesia of Ionia—was the scene of the great victory gained by the two Scipios in B.C. 190, over Antiochus the Great though aided by the Gauls, which handed over Western Asia to the Romans. Hence, in the Mithradatic war, the Magnesians stood firmly by Rome. A coin of this place has on it the head of Cicero, and is interesting as the only portrait (good or bad) we have of that great orator. In legendary history, Mount Sipylus, which overhangs Magnesia on the S., was famous as the residence of Tantalus and Niobe; and here, too, was a town of the same name as the mountain, said to have been converted into a lake by volcanic action[32] (Paus.). Homer alludes to the mountain in speaking of Niobe's transformation (Il. xxiv. 614), as do also Sophocles (Antig. v. 822), and Ovid (Metam. vi. 310). The story of the weeping Niobe was probably an optical illusion (Paus. Attic. c. 21), and, curiously, the origin of it has been clearly shown by Chandler, who says, "The phantom of Niobe may be defined as an effect of a certain portion of light and shade on a part of Sipylus, perceivable at a particular point of view. The traveller, who shall visit Magnesia after this information, is requested to observe carefully a steep and remarkable cliff, about a mile from the town; varying his distance, while the sun and shade, which come gradually on, pass over it, I have reason to believe he will see Niobe" (Travels, p. 331). The magnetic influence on the compass is confirmed by Arundell, but the name "Magnet" has been derived from other towns of the same name.

> 32. Hamilton (vol. i. p. 49) confirms the identity of Sipylus and its neighbourhood with the legend of Tantalus, by the discovery of his friend Mr. Strickland (it had been previously, however, noticed by Chishull) of a remarkable statue sculptured on the rocky base of the mountain. "This statue" Mr. Strickland states, "is rudely sculptured out of the solid rock. It represents a sitting figure contained in a niche, and its height from the base to the top of the head may be about twenty feet." "There can be little doubt that this is the ancient statue of Cybele mentioned by Pausanias," but it can scarcely be, as some other travellers have supposed, Niobe.

PHILADELPHIA, named from Attalus Philadelphus, suffered more than any other Lydian town from earthquakes, so that, after that in the reign of Tiberius it was well-nigh deserted. It continued, however, to hold its own for many years, and is memorable for the long and gallant resistance it made to the Turks. It submitted, at length, in A.D. 1390, to Bayazíd, and is still a place of some size under its new name of Allah-Shehr. Philadelphia is noticed in the Revelations (iii. 7) as one of the Seven Churches. A story long prevailed of a wall made of bones of the citizens slain by Bayazíd; and Rycaut remarks, that "these bones are so entire that I brought a piece thereof with me from thence." Chandler, however, found a simple solution for this wonder in a petrifying stream, like that at Laodicea. "This," says he, "encrusted some vegetable substances which have perished, and left behind, as it were, their moulds." Gibbon particularly notices the gallantry of the Philadelphians:— "At a distance," says he, "from the sea, forgotten by the Emperor, encompassed on all sides by the Turks, her valiant citizens defended their religion and freedom above fourscore years, and, at length, capitulated with the proudest of the Ottomans in 1390. Among the Greek colonies and Churches of Asia, Philadelphia is still erect, a column in a scene of ruins."

TRALLES, in the time of Strabo, was one of the most flourishing cities of Asia Minor; indeed, situated as it was, on the high road from Ephesus through Lydia and Phrygia, it could hardly have failed to be a place of great traffic (Cic. Ep. ad Att. v. 14; Artemid. ap. Strab. xiv. p. 663). Hence its citizens were generally selected to fill the expensive offices of Asiarchs, or Presidents of the games celebrated in the province. Though abundant ruins may be seen over the whole site of the ancient city, they have been so shattered by earthquakes as to be now scarcely recognizable.

We come now to SARDES, by far the most important city of Lydia. The date of its foundation has not been recorded, but it must have early been a place of note, as Herodotus states that it was plundered by the Cimmerians, though they could not capture its citadel.[33] Its real importance, however, evidently began when it became the capital of the Lydian monarchs, men whose unusual wealth has been fully attested by Herodotus, who had himself seen the gifts of Crœsus in the treasury at Delphi. The story of the mode whereby the citadel of Sardes was taken by Cyrus is most likely true; indeed is, in some degree, confirmed by a later capture, under circumstances not unsimilar, by Lagoras, a general of Antiochus the Great (Polyb. vii. 4-7).

33. Sardes, from Σάρδεις; but it is often written Sardis.

Under the reign of Crœsus, Sardes was unquestionably a great and flourishing city, the resort of men of learning and ability, who were, Herodotus tells us, attracted thither by the fame and hospitality of the king (i. 29): on the success of Cyrus, it was simply transferred from the native dynasty of rulers to the conquering Persians, becoming thus, not only the capital of Persian Asia Minor, but the occasional residence of the monarch himself. Thus Xerxes spent the winter there when preparing his unwise invasion of Greece (Herod. vii. 32-37); and here, too, Cyrus the Younger collected the army so easily crushed on the fatal day of Cunaxa. Xenophon remarks that the beauty of its gardens excited the admiration of even the Spartan Lysander, who was amused by the tale that Cyrus himself had often played there the part of gardener (Œcon. p. 880; cf. Cic. de Senect. c. 17). The town itself seems to have consisted chiefly of thatched houses, and so was easily burnt by the Ionians in their revolt. The burning of Sardes was felt by the Persian monarch to be a gross insult, the more so that his rule had been notoriously mild and equitable. Sardes made no resistance to Alexander the Great; hence, its people were permitted by that monarch to retain their ancient laws and customs (Arrian, i. 17). During the wars of the Seleucidæ it was, at different times, subject to the prevailing ruler of that house, and, hence, passed over to the Romans after the defeat of Antiochus at Magnesia.[34] Colonel Leake has given, in his Asia Minor, some interesting notes by Mr. Cockerell on the antiquities of this town, with a special account of the famous temple of Cybele, or the Earth, which stood on the banks of the Pactolus, and of which three great columns were then standing.[35] This temple was burnt by the Ionians in B.C. 503, and never completely reconstructed.[36] Most interesting to the Christian are the remains of two churches, one supposed to be that of the Church of the Panagia, and another, in front of it, said to be that of St. John. The former is almost wholly constructed of magnificent fragments of earlier edifices, and is, perhaps, as Colonel Leake thought, "the only one of the Seven churches of which there are any distinguishable remains." Bearing in mind, too, St. Paul's residence for three years in the neighbouring town of Ephesus, we must suppose the capital of Lydia was included in the declaration of St. Luke that "all they which dwelt in Asia (*i.e.* Roman Proconsular Asia) heard the word of the Lord Jesus, both Jews and Greeks" (Acts xix. 10; compare also 1 Cor. xvi. 19, and Rev. iii. 1-5). In later days, more than one Council was held here. Indeed, this famous city may be traced through a long period of Byzantine history (Eunap. p. 154; Hierocl. p. 669). The emperor Julian made Chrysanthius, of Sardes, pontiff of Lydia; but his attempt to restore the heathen worship was a failure. About A.D. 400 it was plundered by the Goths under Tribigild and Cainas, officers in Roman pay; in the eleventh century it was seized by the Turks, and, two centuries later, nearly destroyed by Tímúr. A miserable village, called Sart, now occupies its site; and so completely has it passed away, that we might inquire with Horace, "Quid Crœsi regia Sardes?" if we may not quite add the commencement of the following line, "Smyrna quid?" (Horat. Epist. I. i. 2). No remains of its ancient grandeur now exist, and the "princes" of Lydia, her wise men, her captains, and "her rulers and her mighty men" have long been asleep in the innumerable tumuli spread over all the level country around.

> 34. A part of the fortifications of Sardes bore the same name, Prion, which we find at Ephesus (Polyb. vii. 4-7). Is the name in any way connected with Priene? As a Greek word, πρίων means a saw; hence, possibly, a serrated ridge of hills—the Spanish *sierra*.
>
> 35. There are only two now (Arundell).
>
> 36. Colonel Leake, in 1824, supposed the Temple of Ephesus was the largest temple of antiquity. It is now known that it was really the sixth in size—that of Agrigentum in Sicily being the largest.

We proceed now to notice some of the more important towns of CARIA, and take first HALICARNASSUS (now Budrum) which had achieved the most enduring fame, as the site of the Mausoleum or Tomb of Mausolus, once of the Seven Wonders of the World. Originally, a colony from Trœzene, in Argolis, Halicarnassus had early adopted Asiatic tastes and habits; hence, firmly adhering to the Persians, its Queen Artemisia I., the widow of Lygdamis, fought for Xerxes at Salamis. A remarkable vase in Egyptian alabaster, with the name and titles of Xerxes on it in the three forms of the cuneiform writing, discovered by Mr. Newton in the Mausoleum, was, perhaps, the reward-gift of the Persian monarch for this service. To her namesake, the second Artemisia, we owe the building of the Mausoleum, 130 years subsequently.

With regard to the history of this remarkable monument, it is well known that, on the death of Mausolus, B.C. 353, Artemisia, his widow and sister, resolved to celebrate his memory by all the honours the art and literature of the period could bestow, and to employ, for this purpose, four of the most celebrated sculptors of antiquity,—Bryaxis, Timotheus, Leochares or Scopas, and Praxiteles.[37] It is said that this queen's short reign, of two years only, did not enable her to witness the completion of her grand design, but that these great sculptors finished the work after her death for their own honour and the glory of art. Much of what they accomplished was, certainly, extant till comparatively modern times. Thus, the building is noticed, first by Strabo and Pliny, then by Gregory of Nazianzus in the fourth, by Constantinus Porphyrogenitus in the tenth, and by Eudocia in the eleventh centuries respectively; all these accounts implying that it was still visible. Again, Frontanus, the historian of the siege of Rhodes, states that a German knight, Henry von Schlegelholt, constructed the citadel at Budrum out of the Mausoleum. Yet, even then, it was only partially destroyed, for when Cepio visited Budrum in 1472 he mentions seeing its remains among the ruins of the ancient town. In the later repairs, however, of the citadel, the masonry of the substructure of the Mausoleum must have been wholly removed; the result being that visitors to Budrum, before Mr. Newton commenced his excavations, could not determine its site.

> 37. Its architects were Satyrus and Phiteus, and the building itself a parallelogram surrounded by thirty-six columns, supporting a pyramid of twenty-four steps, which tapered to the top like a *meta*, or goal. Its height was 140 feet. Martial describes it as "Aere vacuo pendentia Mausolea." Pausanias states that the Romans admired it so much that they called all similar buildings "Mausolea"; while Eustathius, in the twelfth century, observes of it, Θαῦμα καὶ ἦν καὶ ἔστι ("it was and is a wonder") clearly implying its existence, in some form or other, even then. In M. Guichard's "Funérailles de Romains," &c., Lyons, 1581,

the sculptured reliefs and "certain white marble steps" (possibly those of the pyramid) are noticed. This information, he says, he had from M. Dalechamps—the editor of Pliny—and he, again, from M. de la Tourette, who was present, in 1522, when its last stones were finally removed to build the castle.

About the middle of the last century, the Greek sculptures built into the walls of the fortress were published in Dalton's "Views in Greece and Egypt, 1751-81," and were subsequently described by Choiseul-Gouffier, Moritt, Prokesch von Osten, W. J. Hamilton, as, also, in the second volume of "Ionian Antiquities." Nothing, however, was done towards a more complete examination of them, till, in 1845, Sir Stratford Canning (now Lord Stratford de Redcliffe), then H.M. Ambassador at Constantinople, was able to extract them from these walls, and to present them to the British Museum in February, 1846. The chief subject of these sculptures is the contest between the Greeks and the Amazons, and their artistic style may be compared with that of the slabs on the Choragic monument of Lysicrates at Athens, of the date of B.C. 334. The pieces thus recovered were evidently but subordinate portions of a much larger design.

From this time nothing further was done till Mr. Newton was sent by Lord Stratford de Redcliffe, in the early part of 1856, on a cruise to the south of the Archipelago; on which occasion he landed at Budrum, and partially examined the site, but without detecting any visible evidence of the Mausoleum.[38] In October of the same year, however, Mr. Newton took up his abode at Budrum with a few sappers under the command of Lieut. Smith, R.E. Mr. Newton commenced his excavations on the same spot he had previously slightly examined, and, for some time, met with little except abundant mosaics, the remains of a splendid villa, some of them inscribed with the names of the persons represented,—such as Meleager and Atalanta, Dido and Æneas. A little further on, Mr. Newton found in the rubble several drums of columns, with late and shallow Doric flutings, and, at one corner of the building, a well, in which was a small head in white marble, a bronze lamp, and some other objects: many, too, of the rooms still retained their skirting of white marble. But still no Mausoleum appeared.

> 38. Admiral Spratt, R.N., a veteran surveyor, proposed his site for the Mausoleum, because, 1. he thought it coincided with the description of Vitruvius; 2. on the eastern side there are still portions of an Hellenic wall; 3. on the N. side were several fragments of columns of large diameter; and, 4. it might be inferred that the Mausoleum stood on a mound. He did not, however, follow the example of Prof. Ross, in writing a paper against Mr. Newton's early account of the Mausoleum in the "Classical Museum," with a sneer at the possibility of any student, who had not himself surveyed the place, forming a

conception of the real position of the great building. It is satisfactory to know that Prof. Ross's personal survey proved to be even less satisfactory than that of Capt. Spratt.

At length, however, Mr. Newton commenced digging on a spot where, nearly sixty years ago, Professor Donaldson had noticed the remains of "a superb Ionic edifice," and soon came on many small fragments of a frieze in high relief, and on a portion of a colossal lion resembling in execution the lions' heads built into the walls of the castle. Mr. Newton next fell in with a mass of ruins lying just below the surface, one column, indeed, standing nearly upright but inverted, and 10 feet below, a little further on, with the edge of a pavement or step, about 6 inches below which the native rock had been levelled for a floor. In the earth on this floor was found the body of a colossal statue from the waist to the ankle, and another mass of sculpture—a warrior on horseback in a Persian or Oriental costume, in itself a most remarkable specimen of ancient sculpture. There could be no doubt now that these were relics of the Mausoleum, the smoothed rock being the bed on which the building had once stood. The work, in all cases, was of the best, the fragments of the small figures being generally better preserved than those on the frieze already in the British Museum. The discovery of the column just alluded to had this especial value, that, by its measurement and order, a judgment could be formed of the size of the building to which it had belonged: ultimately these measurements showed that the building itself must have had much resemblance in style to the temple at Priene.

By the spring of the next year (1857) Mr. Newton had determined the base-lines of the original building, and proved it must have been a parallelogram 116 feet long on the west by 126 feet on the south side, its entire circumference having been about 472 feet. The inner part of this quadrangle was paved with large slabs of a greenish-grey stone 1 foot thick. The cause of the ruin of the building was, also, clear enough; first, earthquakes shook down a considerable portion, and then the Knights of Rhodes, and, after them, the Turks, used up every available stone above ground for building purposes. Fortunately, however, the plunderers only took what was ready to their hand; hence the massive courses of the foundation-stones were left, because unseen. On the western side, a grand staircase of twelve steps, 30 feet wide, led from the base of the hill to the western side of the precincts of the Mausoleum. Near these were found the vase of Xerxes, and a gigantic stone weighing more than ten tons, which probably once closed the entrance to the actual tomb. No remains of the tomb itself were found; yet, there is reason for believing that some portion of it, if not the actual body of the king, was visible during the demolition by the Knights. On the east side of the Mausoleum, a colossal seated male figure was next discovered, of a grand style, but sadly shattered; and then, on the north, a similarly colossal female figure, which must have been originally scarcely less than 12 feet high. Here, also, was found a very beautiful fragment of one of the friezes, representing a female figure stepping into a chariot, the face of which, happily but slightly injured, retains even now the finish of a cameo.

Mr. Newton's next plan of ascertaining, if possible, the boundary-wall of the *temenos* was a happy one, as he thus, at once, discovered a mass of marble blocks, piled one above another, and intermixed with fragments of statues; and thus unearthed, (1) a colossal horse, in two pieces, and part of the head of another horse, with the bronze bridle still adhering to it; (2) a lion in fine condition, and another in two pieces; (3) a draped female figure broken in half; (4) a head of Apollo. All these sculptures were found heaped together, and had evidently not been disturbed since they had fallen.

The conclusion was inevitable, that parts of the colossal horses of the quadriga from the top of the monument had now been met with; and that this quadriga and much of the pyramid, its support, had been simply hurled upon and over the wall of the *temenos*, and that Mr. Newton had, in fact, found them just as they had fallen, it may be 1,700 years ago.[39] Near to the horse's head, too, was found a face of a colossal male head, presumably that of some personage connected with the quadriga, and, from its general style, which is analogous to the idealized portrait of Alexander the Great on the coins of Lysimachus, most likely from a statue of Mausolus himself. The face has a noble expression, and by a happy accident, the outlines of the features have remained uninjured. Though we have no actual evidence on this subject, it is probable that the statue we have called Mausolus was standing in the chariot at the top of the monument. On the south side of the building Mr. Newton found several portions of what, when put together, were clearly parts of one of its wheels. The fragments consisted of part of the outer circle, half the nave, and a piece of one of the spokes. The wheel, originally, had six spokes, the alternate intervals between each spoke having been closed to ensure by its solidity the strength of the whole wheel. As what has been found shows that the wheel was 7.7 inches in diameter; and as the horses could scarcely have been less than 10 feet in length, we may fairly suppose the top of the pyramid on which the quadriga stood was at least 24 feet long. From other calculations it may be shown that the pyramid was 23½ feet high: but for these and other similar details we must refer our readers to Mr. Newton's work on the Mausoleum.

> 39. It is reasonable to conjecture that the first ruin of the Mausoleum was due to the earthquakes of the first and second centuries A.D., to which we have already alluded.

We must, however, add that the measurements of the height and tread of the blocks of marble believed to have been the steps of the pyramid, formed an essential feature of the calculation. The results arrived at were mainly due to the ingenuity and mathematical knowledge of Lieut. Smith, R.E., who was also able to distribute Pliny's 36 columns over a circumference of 412 feet, so as to preserve a uniform intercolumniation on each side of the building.

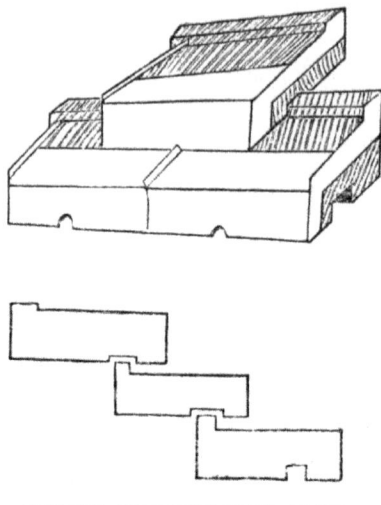

STEPS OF THE PYRAMID.

The difficulty of Lieutenant Smith's theory is that so large a space from the centres of the columns to the walls of the cella is left unsupported; but the plan of support he has suggested occurs in other and nearly contemporaneous structures, as, for instance, in a tomb at Mylasa. Again the great height, 65 feet, between the bases of the columns and the ground, is found to agree with the proportions of other tombs, as in Lycia and at Souma in Algeria. In all probability, this lofty basement was ornamented by one or more friezes, while the lions, of which Mr. Newton found remains of no less than fourteen, may have stood between the columns or at the corners, looking out on the plain. Since their arrival in England, great skill has been shown in uniting the innumerable fragments into which some of the slabs and statues had been broken; and visitors to the British Museum are now able to form a good idea of the grandeur and beauty of the equestrian or Amazonian figure, whose costume resembles that of the Persians on the temple of the Wingless Victory at Athens; and of the two great statues it has been agreed to call Mausolus and Artemisia. In the same room, there may, also, now be seen the whole of the frieze that has been recovered; and it is interesting to observe how much less injured are the portions excavated by

Mr. Newton, than those which, built into the castle wall, have for four centuries, at least, been exposed to the corroding action of the sea-breezes.

We take next CNIDUS, at the S.W. end of Asia Minor, and, after Halicarnassus, the most celebrated city of Caria. The description of its position by Strabo and Pausanias coincides exactly with the observations of modern travellers. Thus, Strabo speaks of its two ports, one of which can be closed; and of an island (now Cape Krio) in front of the city, lofty, in the form of a theatre, and joined by a causeway to the mainland; both of which statements are completely confirmed by Beaufort and Hamilton. Pausanias adds that the island was connected by a bridge. The whole district is covered by ruins, the northern wall being, according to Hamilton, nearly perfect: he adds, that "there is a round tower of great beauty at the extremity of the peninsula, near the northern harbour" (ii. 40). Some of the most important architectural features of the town may be seen in the "Ionian Antiquities."

Cnidus is noticed first in the Homeric hymns, and later as a Lacedæmonian colony, and as a member of the Dorian Hexapolis, or assembly of six cities, whose place of meeting was the temple of the Triopian Apollo, on Cape Krio.[40] As a population, the Cnidians were great traders, combining with this a love for, and a high sense of, art. Thus we find them at a remote period in Egypt (Herod. ii. 178), and possessing a treasury at Delphi, while Lipara, near Sicily, was one of their colonies. In the various wars of the fifth and fourth centuries B.C., we find the Cnidians sometimes on one side and sometimes on the other. Thus, they submitted to Harpagus, the general of Cyrus;[41] then supported Athens, then deserted her after her losses in Sicily,[42] and then, again, in Roman times, were, generally, on the side of Rome.[43] The Cnidians derived much fame from their patronage of art. Thus, the famous painting of Polygnotus in the Lesche at Delphi was their gift;[44] as were also a statue of Jupiter at Olympia, and one at Delphi, of their founder, Triopas; with other statues of Leto, of Apollo, and of Artemis shooting arrows at Tityus. The most famous art-possession of Cnidus was the naked statue by Praxiteles so well known as the Cnidian Venus,[45] of which abundant notices are extant, especially in Lucian. It stood in a chamber with two doors, so that it could be seen all round, and many people visited Cnidus solely for this purpose. So proud were the Cnidians of this statue that, when Nicomedes offered to pay the whole public debt of Cnidus in return for the statue, they preferred keeping their statue and their debts. This statue, justly considered the fittest representation of the "Regina Cnidi Paphique," continued long uninjured, and is mentioned by Philostratus in his life of Apollonius of Tyana; but, in the reign of Theodosius, having been removed to Constantinople, it was totally destroyed by fire in the palace of Lausus, about A.D. 475. There were also preserved at Cnidus two statues by Bryaxis and Scopas, two of the sculptors of the Mausoleum. Cnidus was also famous for her pottery, well known in ancient times by the name of "Κεράμια Κνίδια."[46]

<u>40</u>. Near this temple the Cnidians held their assemblies and the games (ἀγῶνες τοῦ Τριοπίου Ἀπόλλωνος, Herod. i. 144, or Ἀγὼν Δώριος, Arist. ap. Schol. Theocr. Idyll. xvii. 69). The officer in charge of these games was called δαμιουργὸς (Leake, p. 227).

<u>41</u>. The Cnidians wished to cut through the narrow neck of land between their two harbours; but the Delphic oracle replied that, had Jupiter intended Cape Krio should have been an island, he would have made it so:—

Ζεὺς γὰρ κ' ἔθηκε νῆσον εἴ κ' ἐβούλετο—Herod. i. 174.

<u>42</u>. Cnidus paid dear for this desertion by loss of all her ships (Thucyd. viii. 35, 42).

<u>43</u>. Hamilton (ii. 42) shows that more than one of Julius Cæsar's personal friends were connected with Cnidus.

<u>44</u>. See papers by W. W. Lloyd in "Museum of Classical Antiquities," vol. i. 1851.

<u>45</u>. Praxiteles made two statues of Venus, one naked, the other veiled. The Coans chose the latter, the Cnidians the former.

<u>46</u>. The territory round Cnidus was rich in wine, corn, oil, and various vegetables, noticed by Athenæus (i. p. 33, ii. p. 66), and by Pliny (xiii. 35, xix. 32, &c.). Pliny adds (xvi. 64) that Cnidian reeds made excellent pens; hence the fitness of Catullus's lines—

"Quæque Ancona Cnidumque arundinosam

Colis" (Carm. xxx. vi. 11).

The historian Ctesias, Eudoxus, a disciple of Plato, and Agatharcides, were natives of Cnidus. From Hierocles, the Notitiæ and the Acts of Councils, it would seem to have existed as late as the seventh and eighth centuries.

The report of the Dilettanti Society, to which we have alluded, and those of Captain Beaufort and others, having excited much interest in England, it was thought advisable that careful excavations should be made at a spot where there was so much promise of successful results; hence Mr. Newton, at the close of his work at Halicarnassus, resolved to do for Cnidus what he had done for the other Carian city.

DEMETER FROM CNIDUS.

Mr. Newton commenced his operations by examining a platform supported by polygonal masonry, and jutting out like a pier from the side of the mountain, soon discerning that he was on the site of the *temenos* of Demeter, as a niche in the face of the rock above still retained a portion of a dedicatory inscription to that goddess. Shortly afterwards he found a small *stele*, and, near it, the statue noticed by the Dilettanti mission, the head, hands, and feet of which were wanting. Enough, however, remained to show that it had once been a work "of fine style and execution." Inscriptions soon after turned up on the same spot: one of them recording the dedication of an edifice (οἶκος) and of a statue (ἄγαλμα) to Demeter and Persephone, and, what was of far higher interest, the head of the seated figure just noticed, exhibiting a countenance of exquisite beauty, with a most tender and refined expression. This head has recently been specially studied by Professor Brunn, and his paper on it (translated by Mr. Murray, of the British Museum) published in vol. xi. pt. 1 of the Trans. of the Royal Society of Literature. In this paper Professor Brunn traces, with a masterly hand, the intercrossing ideas suggested by the mixed character of Demeter as a wife, a mother, and a widow. "The character," says he, "of mother pervades the whole mythology of Demeter: the mother who, without a husband, lived only for her child; who had to lose her child, and to be filled with anxiety for her; to have her anxiety lessened, but never silenced or removed, by occasional visits from her daughter.... The eye is sunk in the socket, as if physically weary; but anxiety of mind fights against the weariness, and will not yet surrender to it. The look is not sunk, but is directed upwards, only a little less sharply." ... "Can it be," adds the Professor, "only the result of chance that Christian artists have also represented the Madonna wearing the veil? ... In the centre of the Christian religion, also, is the figure of a mother who lives only for her Child and in her Child, who, in the same way, grieves for the loss of her Son, and finds blessedness in the spiritual contemplation of Him. Suppose a Christian artist were to give his Madonna the head of our Demeter, he would certainly not be censured for it."

About the same time Mr. Newton met with two other statues, each of considerable interest: the one representing a female figure with a modius on her head, partially covered by the peplos, and in her right hand a pomegranate; the other, a female statue nearly six feet high, with its body draped to the feet. Its general character is that of an elderly woman wasted with sorrow, with little of that matronly comeliness which, in ancient art, generally characterizes Demeter. From the Homeric hymn to Demeter we learn that the goddess, while wandering in search of her daughter Persephone, was wont to assume the garb of an old woman, and thus traversed the earth for days without tasting food. She is likened, also, to an aged nurse or housekeeper in a regal house, a description well agreeing with this statue. This type of the sorrowing Demeter has not, we believe, been previously recognized in any extant monument of ancient art. A passage, however, in Clemens Alexandrinus (Cohort. ad Gentes, i. 30, ed. Potter) suggests that she was sometimes represented in sculpture under this aspect.

Near the first statue of Demeter, the sitting figure, were several thin nearly decayed sheets of lead, which, on being unrolled, proved to have been inscribed with curses and imprecations in the names of Demeter, Persephone, and other of the infernal gods. Such inscriptions have been occasionally met with before, and are known by the name of *Diræ*.

On pursuing his researches in this *temenos*, Mr. Newton came upon the entrance to a large chamber, full of miscellaneous antiquities, including many bases of former statues, some with remains of stelæ, others with hollowed spaces for the feet of statues. Most of them bore dedications to Demeter in the Doric dialect; and, with them, were many other objects connected with her worship, as three boar pigs, a calathus, and many votive female breasts in marble. The date of these objects is probably, as Mr. Newton suggests, about B.C. 370-320. Below these, again, were layers of lamps, *amphoriskoi*, vessels in Samian ware, hair-pins of bone, bodkins, and glass bottles, all probably Roman. It is likely that this chamber was formerly a treasury connected with one of the temples; and, that it has never been disturbed since it became a ruin is certain from the fact that the edges of the fractured stones are still clean and sharp. It is curious that, besides the marble pigs, the bones of many young pigs were also found, manifest remains of sacrifices to Demeter.

The clearing out of the Theatres did little to reward Mr. Newton's labours; indeed, it soon became but too clear that all, or nearly all, the finer works had long since been removed, probably, like the Venus, to Constantinople.

Hence, shortly afterwards, he gave his chief attention to a thorough examination of the Necropolis, the vast extent of which naturally inspired hopes of important discoveries. This necropolis, the general character of which is very well shown in one of the plates in the "Ionian Antiquities," must in former days have been one of the most striking features of the town. One of the structures still remaining *in situ* was, Mr. Newton observes, not unlike in form to an early Christian church, with a chamber, vestibule, and apse or alcove at the south end. On each side were smaller apses, and, in front of each of them, a marble sarcophagus. The sarcophagi generally exhibit good Roman work of the time of Domitian, but have suffered much by the fall of the roof; they must once have been magnificent specimens of the decorative style of their day, though they exhibit the decay of good taste in the lavish prodigality of ornament with which they have been covered. In the earth around were abundant fragments of Greek inscriptions, nearly all of them decrees of the Senate and people of Cnidus. One of the tombs Mr. Newton considered to have been that of a certain Lykæthus, as an inscription records decrees in his favour, by show of hands (χειροτονία), at the festival of the greater Dionysia, together with the erection of a statue to him at the public expense. There is no satisfactory proof as to when this Lykæthus lived; but his tomb would seem to date from the early Seleucidan period, when Cnidus was a free city.

Having completed the survey of Cnidus itself, Mr. Newton proceeded next to examine the villages in the neighbourhood, the result being the discovery of a colossal lion. Reports of its existence had reached him before, but it was left to Mr. Pullan, the architect of the expedition, to make its actual discovery, at a distance of between three and four miles to the E. of Cnidus, in a position wherein, except by accident, it might have remained unnoticed for another twenty-one centuries. The exact spot where the lion was found may be seen in the Admiralty chart, which shows, on the summit of a cliff, opposite Cape Crio, the ruins of an ancient tomb, which are strewn all around. Below this, some 60 feet, the lion was reposing on a ledge of rock, beneath which, again, is a sheer precipice of 300 feet into the sea. The lion was lying on its right side, and its upper portion had suffered much from exposure to the weather. It had been carved, as well as the base on which it reposes, of one piece of Parian marble, and measures nearly 10 ft. in length, by 6 ft. in height. This noble lion is probably earlier than the Mausoleum, and exhibits a more severe and majestic style than those of the Mausoleum.[47] The removal of the lion was a labour of much toil and difficulty; indeed, could hardly have been accomplished had Mr. Newton not had the aid of some sailors from an English ship of war.

[47]. See Frontispiece.

The tomb itself was a nearly equal square of 39 ft. 2¾ inches, with the remains of a pyramid like that of the Mausoleum.[48] Its present height is about 17 ft.; the four lower feet being composed of immense blocks of marble, supporting eleven courses of travertine. On the west, and most perfect side, a portion of the lower step of the stylobate still remains. No *data* have been obtained of the exact height of the columns once round the monument; but, as, in an angle step, one tread was 13½ inches, and the other only 10½, it is clear that this structure, like the Mausoleum, was oblong. Although the action of an earthquake was probably the primary cause of the ruin of this monumental tomb, there can be no doubt, also, that it has suffered much from plunderers, who, in search for treasure, have torn up as much of the inner pavement as they could move. The jambs of the doorway still exist, and the interior was shaped like a beehive. The top has been closed in by one immense block, and, as its upper side was somewhat broader than the lower, this block must have been dropped into its position, like the bung of a gigantic cask, after the rest of the building was finished. The chamber, itself, exhibits in its sides a series of openings expanding outwards like embrasures—no doubt, θῆκαι, or resting-places for bodies: indeed, on clearing the rubbish away, a number of human bones were met with. Mr. Newton considers this monument can hardly be later than 350 B.C., and that it was built as a monument to many citizens who had fallen in battle. To what period, then, can it be assigned? Probably to either the repulse of the Athenians by the Cnidians in B.C. 412; or to the defeat of the Lacedæmonians by Conon in B.C. 394; and, of the two, it is more likely it was erected in commemoration of the former event, which was one of much glory to the town. To the north and further inland, are two other tombs of precisely similar construction, but inferior in size.

> 48. Mr. Falkener found at Ouran, in Phrygia, a monument he has restored as similar to this Lion-tomb. We wish he had also given a sketch of the ruin as he found it. (Museum Class. Antiq. i. p. 174.)

Having now devoted a considerable space to Halicarnassus and Cnidus, owing to their being, from recent researches, of such high importance, we must notice very briefly the other towns of Caria. The small town of PHYSCUS is chiefly of interest for its magnificent bay and harbour, so well known to modern navigators (under the name of Marmorice), as one of the finest in the world for vessels of the largest size. Possibly it was this very character that led to its being so little noticed in antiquity, as ancient galleys did not value depth of water. The capacity of the bay of Marmorice will be best comprehended, when we remind our readers that Nelson anchored his whole fleet within it, just before the battle of the Nile. Not far from this was CAUNUS, the ancient capital of a population whom Herodotus held were not Carians; indeed, their coins and architecture seem to prove them Lycians.

The site of Caunus has been identified, there being still considerable monumental remains and walls of so-called Cyclopean masonry. The Caunians were an active and high-spirited race, and made a gallant resistance to the Persians, a few years later joining with equal enthusiasm in the great Ionian revolt (Herod. v. 103). Towards the close of the Peloponnesian war we find Caunus constantly mentioned. Having been rejected by the Romans in a petition against Rhodes, they conceived against them the bitterest hatred, and hence carried out with great atrocity the massacre of the Romans planned by Mithradates (Appian, Mithr. c. 23). Caunus was so unhealthy in the summer that "pale-faced Caunians" became a proverb.

STRATONICEA (now Eski-hissar), one of the chief inland towns of Caria and mainly built by Antiochus Soter, derived its name from his wife Stratonice. The great Mithradates married thence his wife Monima. Not far from the town was the famous temple of Jupiter Chrysaorius, the centre of the political union of the Carian states. Stratonicea has been much explored by travellers; and, so early as 1709, Mr. Consul Sherard presented to the Earl of Oxford a book of Greek inscriptions copied by him at various places in Asia Minor. This volume is now in the Harleian collection. The most important monument of the town is the celebrated edict of Diocletian—in Greek and Latin—the first copy of which, by Sherard, is in the volume just mentioned. The late Colonel Leake[49] has shown that its date is about A.D. 303, and its object to direct those engaged in the traffic of provisions not to exceed certain fixed prices in times of scarcity. Fellows states that the names of many of the articles of food enumerated therein are still used by the peasantry of Asia Minor. *Inter alia*, we learn that silken garments were in common use, as Ammianus[50] pointed out, seventy years later; as also the rough coat or *birrhus*, the *caracallis*, or hooded cloak (afterwards adopted by the monks), the Gallic breeches and socks. The late date of the inscription is shown by its barbarous Latinity, above all, by the reduced value of the *drachma* or *denarius*. Thus a denarius appears as the equivalent of a single oyster, or of the hundredth part of a lean goose! The names of the provisions recorded not only indicate the ordinary food of the people, but also the costly dainties of the epicure. Thus several kinds of honey, of hams, of sausages,[51] of salt and fresh-water fish, of asparagus and of beans, are noted. Gibbon has not failed to notice this inscription, though, in his day, it had been very imperfectly copied.

    49. See Trans. Roy. Soc. of Literature, 1st series, 4to. vol. i. p. 181. 1826.

    50. Ammianus was not acquainted with the true origin of silk. He still describes it, as did Virgil and Pliny, as a sort of woolly substance (*lanugo*) combed from a tree in China.

> 51. The derivation of the word "sausage" may not be generally known. "Icicium" means "minced meat"; "salsum icicium," the same salted. From the latter comes the Italian *salsiccio*, the French *saucisse*, and the English sausage. So *jecur ficatum* (Greek, συκωτὸν), hog's liver, derived from the fattening of geese with figs ("pinguibus et ficis pastum jecur anseris albi," Horat. Satir. ii. 8, 88) is preserved in the Italian *fegato* and the modern Greek συκώτι, used for liver in general. It is curious to meet on a decree on the walls of a temple in Caria with *pernæ Menapicæ*, Westphalian hams.

APHRODISIAS was a considerable place, and, at a very late period, as appears from Hierocles, the capital of Caria. It is but little mentioned in ancient history, but Tacitus records that, setting forth decrees of Cæsar and Augustus in its favour,[52] it pleaded before the Senate for the right of sanctuary attached to its temples, when Tiberius was wisely attempting to abridge these injurious immunities. Aphrodisias was chiefly famous for its magnificent Ionic temple of Venus, many columns of which are still standing. They may be seen in the third volume of the "Ionian Antiquities," 1840,[53] and in Mr. Pullan's work.

> 52. "Dictatoris Cæsaris ob vetusta in partes merita et recens Divi Augusti decretum" (Tacit. Ann. iii. 62). An inscription published by Chishull in his Antiq. Asiat. (p. 152), but, we believe, first copied by Sherard, confirms the statement of Tacitus.
>
> 53. The name of Aphrodisias was more than once changed. Thus when Christianity began to prevail, the first change was to Tauropolis (as is shown on an inscription copied by Fellows), and, again, to Stauropolis (or the city of the Cross). When, however, towards the end of the fifth century, the festivals of Venus were revived by Asclepiodotus of Alexandria, the ancient name was revived also.

Sir Charles Fellows has given an excellent description (Lycia, p. 32) of the state in which he found the ruins, with a beautiful drawing of the Ionic temple. "I never," says he, "saw in one place so many perfect remains, although by no means of a good age of the arts": he thinks, too, that the early city must have been in great measure destroyed. "These (the later) walls are," he adds, "composed of the remains of temples, tombs, and theatres removed, although uninjured. The reversed inscriptions, and inverted bas-reliefs bear testimony to this change." Sir Charles Fellows quotes one inscription as showing how carefully the owners of these tombs endeavoured to secure their preservation and sole occupancy. "But if," says the legend, "contrary to these directions, anybody shall bury another (in this monument), let him be accursed, and besides pay into the most holy treasury 5,000 denarii, of which one-third is to be his who institutes the proceedings." Inscriptions with similar curses are, indeed, common enough.

MYLASA *and* LABRANDA may be taken together, as from the former a Sacred Way led to Labranda. The former was, no doubt, in early times one of the chief places in Caria, before Halicarnassus was adopted as the royal residence; indeed, we find a proof of this in the fact that it had a temple to which Lydians and Mysians were alike admitted (Herod, i. 171). Physcus, to which we have already referred was considered as its port. Mylasa, in ancient times, as Strabo avers, a city of great beauty, owed much to its having been built close to a mountain of the finest white marble. It was, indeed, so close, that one of the provincial governors observed that the founder of the town ought to have been ashamed of his blunder, if not frightened.[54] It was, also, so full of sacred buildings, that when Stratonicus came there, thinking there were more temples than people, he exclaimed, in the middle of the forum, "Hear, oh ye temples"! (Athen. viii. p. 348).

54. Strabo's words are: Ταύτην γὰρ, ἔφη, τὴν πόλιν ὁ κτίσας εἰ μὴ ἐφοβεῖτο, ἆρ' οὐδ' ᾐσχύνετο; (xiv. 659).

The people of Mylasa having made a successful resistance to the attacks of Philip, the son of Demetrius, were rewarded by being made "free" by the Romans. Modern travellers, from Pococke to Chandler, fully confirm the statements of the ancients as to the abundance of marble monuments; and Colonel Leake adds that, since they were there, the Turks have pulled down the best ruin, that of the Temple of Romulus and Augustus. Sir Charles Fellows, on his second journey, observed on the key-stone of a gateway the double-headed axe (bipennis), indicating that the building to which it belonged had once been consecrated to the Jupiter of Labranda, a name said to have been derived from λαβρὺς, the Carian word for an axe;[55] and succeeded, also, in identifying it (pp. 66-67). He says of it, "The only conspicuous building of the place is a beautiful temple of the Corinthian order, but I think not of the finest age.... It stands in a recess in the hills, and is consequently not seen without approaching close to it."[56]

55. Strabo calls the temple νεὼς ἀρχαῖος, and Herodotus adds that there was a holy grove of plane-trees near it, ἅγιον ἄλσος πλατανίστων (v. 119). Plutarch (ii. p. 302 A) states that λαβρὺς was the Lydian and Carian word for axe (which we find represented also on the coins of Mausolus and Pixodarus). On one of the Oxford marbles (ii. 12), probably an altar, occur the words Διὸς Λαβραύνδου.

56. Since Sir Charles's visit, this spot has been carefully examined by Mr. Pullan, who states that the building (of which the fifteen columns

still stand) is really of Roman times and work, though engraved (under the auspices of Dr. Chandler) as a Greek temple in the "Ionian Antiquities," vol. i. (Pullan, "Ruins of Asia Minor," p. 26).

CHAPTER III.

Xanthus—Sir Charles Fellows—Telmessus—Patara—Pinara—Myra—Tlos and Antiphellus—Attalia—Perge—Eurymedon—Aspendus—Side—Termessus—Cremna—Sagalassus—Selge—Antioch of Pisidia—Tarsus—Coracesium—Laertes—Selinus—Anemurium—Celenderis—Seleuceia—Corycus—Soli—Adana—Mallus—Mopsuestia—Anazarbus—Issus.

WE come now to *Lycia*, of which many of the most important monuments are now in the Lycian room at the British Museum—for the most part the records of its chief town, XANTHUS—and all procured by Sir Charles Fellows. A few less valuable remains, were, at the same time, obtained from other Lycian towns.

The chief value of the monuments from *Lycia* lies in this, that, while they exhibit many well-executed pieces of sculpture, interesting as a local or provincial rendering of Greek work of the middle of the fourth century B.C., they comprise, also, a few slabs, as, for instance, those from the Harpy tomb, of a genuine Archaic type.

Xanthus, the town from which the greater part of the monuments about to be described have been secured, underwent remarkable vicissitudes of fortune, some of which, it has been thought, are indicated on its sculptures. Originally, it was a Cretan colony settled at or near Xanthus; hence we read, in the Iliad, of Sarpedon and Glaucus, as the leaders of the Lycians in the Trojan army, and of the body of the former being carried back by Sleep and Death to Lycia to be honoured with a *stele* and tomb. Pandarus, too, the celebrated archer, is also a Lycian. On the overthrow of Crœsus, Harpagus, Cyrus's general, was sent to reduce Lycia with a mixed force of Persians, Dorians, and Ionians; the Glaucidæ, or royal family of Lycia, having vigorously supported the Ionians in their resistance to Cyrus.

On this occasion Xanthus made a memorable defence. It is said that, when driven from the plain by the united forces of the Persian and confederate army, its people took refuge in their citadel, and, collecting therein their wives, children, and treasures, burnt them, at the same time falling to a man in a furious sally upon their enemies (Herod, i. 176). That the Persian success was complete, we know from the fact, that, sixty years later, the then Xanthians sent fifty ships to the aid of Xerxes, and continued, subsequently, to pay an annual tax to the Persian monarchs.[57] Yet their courage was not subdued; for when Alexander, after his victory over the Persians at the Graneicus, descended into Lycia, at Xanthus, and there alone, he met with an obstinate resistance.

57. It has been suggested (see Rawlinson's Herodotus, i. p. 312) that the family of Harpagus continued to govern Lycia, and that the Xanthian obelisk (to which we shall presently refer) was erected soon after the battle of Eurymedon, B.C. 466. But "son of Harpagus," on that monument, may easily mean no more than his descendant, just as Jehu was called "the son of Omri."

In the subsequent war, the Xanthians supported Antigonus; hence the assault and capture of the town by Ptolemy; and, during the war between Brutus and the Triumvirs, the former entered Lycia, and a bloody attack on, and siege of, Xanthus were the natural results. We are told, that on this occasion, the people of the town did as they had done before when assaulted by Harpagus, destroying themselves, their wives, and their children, in a similar holocaust. Subsequently, we hear little of Xanthus, except that it suffered severely from the two great earthquakes in the days of Tiberius and Antoninus Pius. The town of Xanthus was situated on the left bank of the Sirbes[58] or Sirbus, called Xanthus or the Yellow by the Greeks; at a distance of between 6 and 7 miles from the sea. On the highest point was the Acropolis, a Roman work, built chiefly out of the ruins of the older town. On the brow of the hill stood what has been called the Harpy tomb.

58. Dionysius Periegetes testifies to both names:

Σίβρῳ ἐπ' ἀργυρέῳ ποταμῷ ...

and

Ξάνθου ἐπὶ προχοῇσιν ... κ. τ. λ. (v. 847.)

PERSIAN SATRAP SEATED.

The monuments found at Xanthus may be arranged under the head of (1) the so-called Ionic trophy monument,[59] (2) Miscellaneous reliefs, (3) Tombs. The first stands on the east side of the city, and was constructed of white marble on a basement of grey Lycian stone. Two or more friezes had once surrounded it, representing contests between warriors fully armed after the Greek fashion, or more lightly clad in tunics or naked, and wearing helmets. Sir C. Fellows imagines he can recognize, in some cases, the loose-robed bearded Lycians, with their peculiar arms and *curtained* shields,[60] the battle being that in the plains recorded by Herodotus.[61] Asiatics are certainly represented on some of the slabs with the pointed cap or cydaris, while, on other slabs is an attack on the main gate of a strongly-fortified town. On another relief is a Persian satrap seated, with the umbrella, or symbol of sovereignty, over his head, and on other slabs, are indications of a sortie from the city and of its repulse. The city may or may not be Xanthus itself, but, within the walls, are well-known monuments of that town, upright square pillars or *stelæ*, four of which are represented.[62] The "Trophy monument," which has been cleverly restored by Sir Charles Fellows, as a peripteral tetrastyle temple, may be seen in the Lycian room in the British Museum. We regret, however, we cannot accept his view, that the subject of these sculptures is the capture of Xanthus by Harpagus, as this event took place in B.C. 545; while none of these reliefs can be as early as B.C. 400.[63]

> 59. On the whole, it seems most likely that this monument was the sanctuary of some local hero, possibly of the original founder or leader (οἰκιστής or ἀρχηγέτης), like the Theseum at Athens. It might, therefore, have been the Harpageum, or memorial of Harpagus, or of the Harpagi. Mr. Benjamin Gibson has supposed that the "Trophy monument" was intended to commemorate "the conquest of Lycia by the united forces of the Persians and Ionians" (Mus. of Class. Antiq. vol. i. 132); and Mr. Watkiss Lloyd has published an able memoir on it, entitled "Xanthian Marbles—the Nereid Monument."

> 60. This "curtain" was a sort of appendage attached to the lower end of the shield, and was intended to protect the legs from stones. It was called λαισήϊον, and is mentioned in Hom. Il. v. 453:
>
> ἀσπίδας ἐυκύκλους λαισήϊά τε πτερόεντα.
>
> A vase published by Inghirami well represents the usual character of this appendage. Millingen supposes the subject of this vase to be "Antiope leading Theseus to the walls of Themiscyra." (Cf. Müller, Arch. d. Kunst, § 342.)

> 61. Some of these scenes may refer to real events in the history of Xanthus; and the Oriental chief, too, on the "Trophy" monument would seem to be aided by Greek mercenaries.

62. It has been suggested that the so-called *triquetra* on the Lycian coins, consisting of three curved objects, like sickles or elephant-goads, or the *harpa* (ἅρπη) of Perseus, joined in the centre, is emblematic of the name of Harpagus. Such "canting heraldry" (as in the case of *Arpi* in Apulia, and of *Zancle* in Sicily) is not, however, accepted by the best numismatists as of approved Greek use, though possible enough among a semi-Oriental population.

63. The plate on the opposite page must not be considered as more than a possible arrangement of some of the sculptures found.

2. The Miscellaneous reliefs found in and about the Acropolis are chiefly relics of much older buildings; they are generally in the rough, gritty stone of the country, and have some resemblance to early Greek work, especially to the sculptures from Assos. Their chief subjects are a lion devouring a deer, and a satyr, the size of life, running along the ground.

IONIC TROPHY MONUMENT.

3. The Tombs. The tomb-system, so to speak, as developed in Lycia, is a striking characteristic of that province, and has been, therefore, carefully studied by Sir Charles Fellows, who has classed them, according to their forms, under the heads of Obelisk, Gothic, and Elizabethan. The first, as the name implies, is simply a square block surmounted by a cap and cornice; the second and third have lancet-head tops or deep mullioned recesses, respectively. Of the two first the British Museum has excellent specimens; the third was chiefly used for carvings on the face of solid rocks. All alike exhibit imitations of wooden structures with panelled doors, bossed nails, and knockers suspended from lions' mouths. One of these tombs, the so-

called Harpy tomb, from its great curiosity, we must notice somewhat fully. It consists of a square column about 17½ feet high, in one piece of stone, surmounted by a series of bas-reliefs, forming the walls of a square chamber, seven feet each way, and having a small door on its west side. On these walls are representations of Harpies, between whom, in each case, is a group consisting of one seated and one standing figure. There is reason to suppose the subject of these reliefs a local myth, and, as the daughters of a Lycian hero, Pandarus, are said to have been carried off by Harpies, this is not improbably the subject here. Harpies are usually, as here, indicated with the faces, breasts, and hands of women, and with bodies and feet of vultures. It is possible that this *stele* may have been the tomb of some prince of the royal family of Lycia, who claimed descent from the mythical hero, Pandarus. No certain date can be assigned to it; but, had it been executed in Attica instead of Lycia, B.C. 530 would not have been too early for it. In any case, its execution must have preceded the Persian conquest of Lycia.

One of the most interesting of the Gothic tombs is that of a man whose name has been read Paiafa, and who was, probably a satrap of Lycia. The top of this structure much resembles an inverted boat, with a high ridge running along it, like a keel. On each side of the roof is an armed figure in a *quadriga*;[64] on the north side, below the *tympanum*, the Satrap is seated as a judge, his dress and general appearance being the same as that of the Persian on the Trophy monument.

> 64. Herodotus remarks that the people of Bithynia carried two Lycian spears, and had helmets of brass, on the summits of which were the ears and horns of an ox. Cf. also, on coins, the helmet of Eukratides, king of Bactriana.

In concluding these notes on Xanthus, we may allude to some casts from a tomb at Pinara, hard by, carved on the face of the solid rock. Sir Charles Fellows states that, in the centre of this city, there rises a round rocky cliff, speckled all over with tombs, many of them being only oblong holes, and quite inaccessible. One cast gives the representation of a walled city with tombs, towers, gates, and walls; the battlements, on the whole, much resembling the town shown on the "Trophy monument." Another cast gives the interior of the portico of a rock tomb at Tlos, with Bellerophon, one of the heroes of Lycia, triumphing over the Chimæra.

It only remains for us to notice the famous *Inscribed Stele*, the longest inscription yet met with in the Lycian character, and containing a notice of a son of Harpagus, and the names of several Lycian towns. On the north side, between the lines of Lycian characters, is a Greek inscription in twelve hexameter lines,[65] the first from an epigram of Simonides (B.C. 556), and a notice of the achievements of this son of Harpagus. The whole inscription consists of about 250 lines.

> 65. Colonel Leake (Trans. of the Roy. Soc. of Literature, vol. ii. 1844) has given a translation of the twelve lines in Greek, showing that this monument was erected by a certain Datis, called a son of Harpagus. It states that he had gained the highest honours in the Carian games, and had slain "in one day seven heavy-armed soldiers, men of Arcadia." The epigram of Simonides (Anthol. Brunck. vol. i. p. 134) commemorates the battles at Cyprus and on the Eurymedon, B.C. 470. Another conjecture is that the son of Harpagus was called Sparsis (Leake, ibid. p. 32). Colonel Leake thinks the date of the inscription not earlier than B.C. 400.

Over the other towns of LYCIA, TELMESSUS, PATARA, PINARA, MYRA, TLOS, and ANTIPHELLUS, it is not necessary for us to dwell at any great length, the more so that they were not, historically, of great importance, and are to us only interesting for the remains of art still visible on the spot.

TELMESSUS was on the coast, and is now represented by the village of Makri.[66] In ancient times it was famous for the skill of its augurs. Herodotus tells us they were often consulted by the kings of Lydia, and especially by Crœsus; and Arrian ascribes to them a remote antiquity. Their reputation long survived; for Cicero speaks of the town thus:—"Telmessus in Caria est quâ in urbe excellit haruspicum disciplina" (De Divin. i. 41). In early Christian times it had a bishop. Telmessus has been fully described by Dr. Clarke and Sir Charles Fellows. Its monumental remains are almost wholly tombs; but these are, many of them, remarkable for their beauty, as also for the extraordinary labour bestowed on them in cutting them out of the face of the rock. Sir Charles Fellows makes the curious remark, that, though the Greek population of Lycia were mainly Dorians, he did not meet with any tombs or other monuments unquestionably of the Doric order.

> 66. Fellows remarks that the Meio of the maps and of the "Modern Traveller" (supposed, too, by Cramer to be a corruption of Telmessus) is not known in the country.

PATARA, on the left bank of the river Xanthus, was chiefly celebrated for its worship and temples of the Lycian Apollo, known by the appellation of Patareus.[67] According to Herodotus (i. 182), the priestess who delivered it was shut up in the temple every night, but the oracular responses were only occasional. The Pataræan oracle was very ancient, and considered scarcely inferior to that of Delphi. Captain Beaufort, in his account of Karamania, places the remains of Patara[68] near the shore, and notices "a deep circular pit of singular appearance, which may have been the seat of the oracle." Fellows alludes to "a beautiful small temple about the centre of the ruined city," with a doorway "of beautiful Greek workmanship, ornamented in the Corinthian style, and in fine proportion and scale." The port of Patara, which was too small to contain the combined fleet of the Romans and Rhodians under Regillus in the war with Antiochus (Liv. xxxvii. 17) is now completely overgrown with brushwood, &c. The theatre is shown by an inscription to have been built (more probably rebuilt) in the fourth consulate of Antoninus Pius, A.D. 145.

67. Hor. Od. iii. 4, 62: Delius aut Patareus Apollo. Stat. Theb. i. 696:

... Seu te Lyciæ Pataræa nivosis

Exercent dumeta jugis.

Virg. Æn. iv. 143:

Qualis ubi hibernam Lyciam Xanthique fluenta

Deserit, ac Delum maternam invisit Apollo.

On which passage Servius makes the remark that the oracles were delivered alternately,—during the winter months at Patara, and during the summer at Delos.

68. Cicero uses the Ethnic form Pataranus (Orat. in Flacc. c. 32).

PINARA, at the foot of Mount Cragus, was another of the six Lycian towns in which divine honours were paid to the hero Pandarus, Homer's celebrated archer: its name is said to be a Lycian word for a round hill (v. Ἀρτύμνησος, ap. Ptol.; Plin. v. 28; Hierocl. p. 684); and such a hill, pierced everywhere for tombs, Fellows found, as we have stated, in the very centre of it. Such a physical feature would not have been overlooked by any Greeks. He adds that "the whole city appears to be of one date and people," the inscriptions being generally in the Lycian character.[69] The carvings on the rock-tombs here, judging from the drawing he gives (p. 141), are of much interest and beauty.

69. Colonel Leake (Roy. Soc. Lit. i. p. 267) was of the opinion that the Lycian characters were modifications of Archaic Greek.

MYRA, sometimes called Andriace (whence the modern *Andraki*), was, according to Appian, a place of some note, and it is still remarkable for the beauty and richness of its rock-cut tombs (Pullan). The Sacred historian of St. Paul's journeyings writes that, after quitting Sidon and Cyprus, "when we had sailed over the Sea of Cilicia and Pamphylia, we came to Myra, a city of Lycia; and there the centurion found a ship of Alexandria sailing into Italy, and he put us therein" (Acts xxvii. 5, 6). Myra, at a late period, seems to have been the metropolis of the province (Malala, Chron. xiv.; Hierocl. p. 684). A Nicholas, Bishop of Myra, is also mentioned (Const. Porphyr. Themist. 14). Colonel Leake observes that, on the banks of the river by which Lucullus ascended to Myra, are the ruins of a large building, which, from an inscription, appears to have been a granary, erected in the time of Hadrian;[70] and Fellows adds that "the tombs are generally very large, and all appear to have been for families, some having small chambers, one leading to the other, and some highly interesting from their interior peculiarities of arrangement." Many bas-reliefs within the porticos of the tombs still retain their original colour, as may be seen on the casts from them in the British Museum.

> [70]. Beaufort gives a minute description of this building, and states that it is 200 feet long, with walls 20 feet high. The inscription on it, "HORREA IMP. CAESARIS DIVI TRAIANI HADRIANI," &c., proves that it has been a granary: it was divided into seven separate compartments.

TLOS and ANTIPHELLUS, though occasionally mentioned in ancient times, had been well-nigh forgotten till these and other sites were diligently sought out by modern travellers. Leake speaks of the latter as containing a theatre nearly complete, with many catacombs and sarkophagi, some very large and magnificent; and Fellows thinks the tombs here the largest in Lycia. "The rocks for miles round," he says, "are strewn with their fragments, and many hundreds are still standing, apparently unopened."

TLOS, of which we know little more than that it lay on the road to Cibyra, was first accurately determined by Sir Charles Fellows, who considered the original city must have been demolished in very early times, as "finely-wrought fragments are now seen built into the strong walls which have fortified the town raised upon its ruins." The theatre was the most highly-finished he had seen, for the seats were not only of polished marble, but each seat had an overhanging cornice, often supported by lions' paws. An inscription found there records the name of Sarpedon, showing that the name of the mythical hero of Lycia was still preserved among the people. The name for tomb at Tlos is always Heroum.

As the provinces are so closely connected, we shall take *Pamphylia* and *Pisidia* together, simply selecting from them such sites as seem of the highest interest. We shall, therefore, notice first ATTALIA (the modern Adalia), although there has been some dispute among geographers whether Adalia does really occupy the site of the old city: the true course of a stream called Catarrhactes,[71] from its plunging headlong over precipices into the sea, being still undetermined, has mainly led to this confusion. The probability is that, owing to the agency of earthquakes, the coastline has been much changed during the last 2,000 years; moreover, Colonel Leake and others believe the calcareous matter brought down, in this period by the different streams, sufficient to cause the cessation of any such cascade, the main stream having been also much diverted to fertilize the gardens round the town. The physical changes have in fact, been so great, that it is more wonderful that anything can be determined on a certain and satisfactory basis. Captain Beaufort thought the modern town occupied the site of Olbia.[72] On the other hand, Leake considered Adalia the representative of Attalia, and that Olbia would probably be found in some part of the plain which extends for seven miles from the modern Adalia to the foot of Mount Solyma. Attalia derived its name from Attalus Philadelphus. From it, St. Paul and St. Barnabas, on their return, sailed to the Syrian Antioch (Acts xiv. 25). In later times it was the seat of a bishopric. It is now the principal southern Turkish port of Asia Minor, and has many ancient remains. Leake remarks on "the walls and other fortifications, the magnificent gate or triumphal arch, bearing an inscription in honour of Hadrian, an aqueduct, and the numerous fragments of sculpture and architecture." Fellows adds:—"Adalia, which is called by the Turks *Atalia*, I prefer to any Turkish town that I have yet visited; every house has its garden, and consequently the town has the appearance of a wood, and of what?—orange, lemon, fig, vine, mulberry, all cultivated with the artificial care of a town garden, and now (April 3) in fresh spring beauty." It was from Attalia, or from its neighbourhood, that Mark "turned back"[73] (Acts xiii. 13).

> 71. Colonel Leake remarks that, after heavy rains, the river precipitates itself copiously over the cliffs near the projecting point of the coast, a little to the west of Laara.
>
> 72. "The delightful situation of this place," says he, "appears to have been clearly alluded to in the ancient name Olbia, derived from the adjective ὄλβιος, blessed or happy" (Karamania, p. 137).
>
> 73. Mr. Davis notices the great gate, the inside of it being "ceiled" with small squares of fine white marble and bearing the curious inscription, τὸ ἔργον τῆς πλακώσεως τῆς πύλης—Πλάκωσις does not occur in classical Greek; but πλάξ is a flat surface, and πλακόω is to cover with such pieces. Hence, πλακώτης μαρμάρου is one who overlays with marble. In the commencement of their journey Attalia is not mentioned by name, but only Perga (Acts xiii. 13).

Nearly due N. of Attalia was PERGE, famous in olden times for the temple and worship of Artemis Pergæa.[74] The date of the city is uncertain, but it lasted, as an ecclesiastical centre, till late in the Byzantine times. Alexander, in his march eastwards, occupied Perge, finding, as might have been expected, much difficulty in his advance through the adjacent mountains; St. Paul, too, and St. Barnabas were here twice; first, on their way from Cyprus;

and, secondly, on their return to Syria. The ruins noticed by General Köhler, at a place called *Eski Kalesi*, were probably those of this place. The theatre and stadium are still quite perfect. On these walls and other buildings the Greek shield is constantly carved, reminding the spectator of the passage in Ezekiel, xxvii. 11, "They hanged their shields upon thy walls round about."

74. Perge is mentioned in Callimachus's Hymn to Diana, v. 187:

Νήσων μὲν Δολίχη, πολίωνδέ τοι εὔαδε Πέργη;

and in Dionysius Periegetes, v. 854:

Ἄλλαι δ' ἐξείης Παμφυλίδες εἰσί πόληες

Κώρυκος, Πέργη τε, καὶ ἠνεμόεσσα Φάσηλις.

Passing along the coast to the east we come to the EURYMEDON, physically a small stream, yet celebrated in history for the double defeat, on one and the same day, of the Persians by Cimon. The Persian ships were drawn up at the mouth of the river, but, at the first attack, the crews fled to the shore. Cimon then landed his men, and after a severe struggle the camp and baggage were taken (Thucyd. i. 100; Plut. Vit. Cimon.). Some years later, a Rhodian fleet anchored off its mouth before attacking the fleet of Antiochus, then commanded by Hannibal (Livy, xxxvii.). The entrance of this stream is now completely blocked up by a bar.[75]

75. Dr. Arnold has shown that, in the account in Thucyd. i. 100, the phrase διέφθειραν τὰς πάσας ἐς τὰς διακοσίας means that the number of the ships destroyed by the Athenians was, in all, 200, not that there were no more, as some writers have supposed.

On the Eurymedon was seated the old Argive town of ASPENDUS, some of the coins of which read, barbarously, ΕΣΤΓΕΔΝΥΣ. Thucydides speaks of it as a seaport; but he, probably, means that it was a boat-station at the mouth of the river. Aspendus is noticed by Arrian, and was the place where Thrasybulus was slain in his tent by the natives; it is also mentioned in the campaign of Manlius (Liv. xxxviii.; Polyb. xxii.).[76] Mr. Pullan gives a beautiful drawing of its theatre, which is by far the most perfect in Asia Minor. One other place of considerable reputation in Pamphylia must be briefly noted; viz. SIDE, a colony of the Cumæans of Æolis, and remarkable for the fact that, soon after they came there they forgot their native Greek tongue, and spoke a barbarous jargon. It was off this town the battle was fought when the fleet of Antiochus, under Hannibal, was utterly routed by the Rhodians. When, somewhat later, the pirates of Cilicia became so formidable, Side was one of their chief harbours, and one of the markets where they disposed of their ill-gotten plunder. Side was in Roman times the capital of *Pamphylia prima*, and was still in existence when Hierocles wrote. Capt. Beaufort found it utterly deserted; but its remains would seem to be very striking, especially its outer walls and theatre, which is not less than 409 feet in external diameter, with a perpendicular height, from the area, of 79 feet: all its seats are, Capt. Beaufort says, of white marble, and the building could have held 13,370 persons, sitting comfortably; it is, he adds, "in a very perfect state; few of the seats have been disturbed, even the stairs are, in general, passable." The same observer considered that, at some later period, this great structure had been converted into a fortress, as walls, with towers and gates, but of inferior work, now extend to the seashore.

76. From Dionys. Perieg. 852, it would seem that Venus had a peculiar worship there—for ἔνθα συοκτονίῃσι Διωναίην ἱλάονται.

Our knowledge of the ancient geography of *Pisidia* is mostly derived from Arrian's notice of Alexander's march, from Livy's account of the expedition of C. Manlius Vulso, and from the details in Polybius of the hostilities carried on by Garsyeris, the general of Achæus, against the people of TERMESSUS, one of its chief cities. At the time Manlius was approaching this town the Termessians were in open war with the people of Isionda or Isinda, and, having captured this city, were besieging the citadel. The Roman general was not sorry to have so good a pretext for interfering; hence his march on Isinda, his relief of that city, and his fining the Termessians fifty talents. A glance at the map suggests that he must have come in, by the defiles of Milyas, near a place now called Al-Malu. The presumed ruins of Isinda have been noticed by M. Coransez, as extending over nearly a square league, and as remarkable for their massive structure.

TERMESSUS itself was evidently at the entrance of the defiles whereby Pisidia communicates with Pamphylia and Lycia. Arrian says that "the men of Termessus occupy a site very lofty and precipitous on every side, the road passing close to the city being very difficult, as the mountain reaches down from the city to the road. There is over against this, another mountain not less precipitous, and these form a gate, as it were, on the road," &c. This statement is fully confirmed by the observation of General Köhler (ap. Leake, Asia Minor, pp. 133-135): "The two great ranges on the west and north of the plains of Adalia," says he, "now approach each other, and, at length, are only divided by the passes through which the river finds its way. The road, however, leaves this gorge to the right, and ascends the mountain by a paved and winding causeway, a work of great labour and ingenuity."[77] Alexander the Great, it would seem, despaired of taking the town; or, possibly, thought its siege would detain him too long; he, however, forced the defiles, passing on to the north to Cormasa, Cremna, and Sagalassus, a course probably pursued by Manlius subsequently.[78] CREMNA, where, owing to its great natural strength, the Romans placed a colony (Strab. xii.

569), has been carefully examined by Mr. Davis ("Anatolica," p. 182), who gives also a plan, showing the construction of this remarkable fortress. His description is as follows:[79] "It (Kremna) is a plateau of limestone, which is bounded on three sides by precipices, some extremely deep and abrupt."

77. There is some confusion between the two Termessi, one of which is apparently to the left of the road passing W. and N.W. from Adalia. This we think was *Termessus Minor*—the *Almalu* of Mr. Davis. The more important place, *Termessus Major* (on its coins μείζων), was at the head of the pass described. These views are confirmed by Eustath. and Dion. Perieg. v. 858, Stephan. Byzant., and Hierocles. At a later period, the see of Termessus had united with it the churches of two other places—Jovia and Eudocia.

78. Cramer and some other geographers place Cremna to *the* N. as well as the E. of Sagalassus, where it *could not have been*.

79. The description in Arundell, vol. ii. pp. 59, &c., shows that he had explored the same ruins forty years before Mr. Davis, under the idea they were those of Selge, though, on his plate, he adds the words, "Acropolis of Germe—Cremna." Colonel Leake, too, suggested that "Germe" was perhaps a corruption of "Cremna." Had Mr. Arundell reflected on an inscription he himself copied there ... ΛΔΗ ... ΝΑΤΩΝ, he might have seen that the last word could naturally be supplied as ΚΡΗΜΝΑΤΩΝ—"of the people of Kremna." Zosimus says the winding path up to the fortress was called by the natives the *Snail*.

"From it," he adds, "the country inclined rapidly in its general formation to the valley of the Kestrus, which must have been at least 5,000 feet below us.... Most of the buildings of the city lay to the N.W. of our point of ascent. On the N.E. and N. was an extensive open space cultivated, but with many oak trees and with much underwood scattered over it." ... Zosimus (A.D. 425) relates the history of the blockade of Kremna by a Roman army. It had been occupied by Lydius, an Isaurian free-booter, and his provisions falling short, he caused a part of the plateau to be sowed with corn. A great double gate is the only structure still standing, and, as all the columns have fallen exactly in the same direction, Mr. Davis reasonably conjectures they were overthrown by a single shock of an earthquake. Some well-paved streets are traceable, one 18 feet wide, with tombs and corridors running along each side. It is curious that a place so remarkable, physically, is scarcely mentioned by ancient writers. Thus, it is not noticed in the campaign of Alexander, who must have passed under it, but it was taken by Strabo's contemporary, the Galatian Amyntas (xii. 569),[80] and was still later, as we have stated, a Roman colony with the title "Colonia Julia Augusta Cremna." Its name is obviously derived from κρημνός, an overhanging precipice.[81] Kremna was a Christian bishopric, but only one of its bishops, Theodorus, is recorded.

> 80. Ἀμύντας ... πολλὰ χωρία ἐξεῖλεν, ἀπόρθητα πρότερον ὄντα, ὧν καὶ Κρῆμνα (Strab. xii. 569).

> 81. Zosimus's description is exactly to the point:—Κρῆμναν ... ἐν ἀποκρήμνῳ τε κειμένην καὶ κατὰ μέρος χαράδραις βαθυτάταις ὠχυρωμένην (i. c. 69).

SAGALASSUS was taken by Alexander, after a severe conflict, the result being, says Arrian, that all the rest of Pisidia submitted to his arms (i. 28). On the other hand, Manlius contented himself with ravaging the territory around it; thereby compelling the Sagalassians to pay a heavy contribution both of money and produce. Both Arrian and Livy bear testimony to the warlike and independent character of the mountaineers of this part of Asia Minor; while Strabo adds that it passed over to the Romans, as one of the towns of Amyntas, the tetrarch of Lycaonia. Sagalassus is further noticed by Pliny and Ptolemy, and, in Christian times, was a bishopric. Some magnificent ruins, at a great height above the plain, have been proved by Mr. Arundell to be those of this place, as he found there an inscription reading ΣΑΓΑΛΑΣΣΕΩΝ ΠΟΛΙΣ ΤΗΣ ΠΙΣΙΔΙΑΣ, "The City of the Sagalassians of Pisidia." The position of the old town, as may be seen in one of the engravings in Mr. Arundell's second Journey, is exceedingly picturesque; and we may feel sure Arrian is correct in stating that Alexander encountered a stiff resistance from its inhabitants ere he forced his way into the town.

The existing remains of Sagalassus are mostly Roman, but there is one very old wall of polygonal masonry. One of the principal ruins, with a portico 300 feet long by 27 feet wide, has probably been a Christian church: there is, also, a singularly perfect theatre. The ruins of the Christian church exhibit a building of vast proportions, constructed of huge blocks of marble, with Corinthian columns two feet in diameter. A large cross is cut deep into one of the blocks at the principal entrance. Mr. Hamilton, who calls the modern village Allahsún, says that "there is no other ruined city in Asia Minor, the situation and extensive remains of which are so striking, or so interesting, or which give so perfect an idea of the magnificent combination of temples, palaces, theatres, gymnasia, fountains, and tombs which adorned the cities of the ancient world."[82]

> 82. Hamilton adds—"To the south is a high, insulated, and conical hill, agreeing with Arrian's description of the Acropolis, λόφος πρὸ τῆς πόλεως—a hill in front of the city."

One other place in Pisidia we have yet to mention, SELGE, of old one of its chief cities, yet, strange to say, at present unidentified, or only so doubtfully.

Originally a colony from Lacedæmon, Selge maintained throughout its whole history the character of its founders, and, probably, owing to better laws and government, soon surpassed all the neighbouring towns in population and power, Strabo believing that it once had as many as 20,000 inhabitants. Much of its success was due to the security of its position, high among the mountains and difficult of access. Hence, the Selgians retained their personal freedom, and, though more than once compelled to pay heavily and deservedly for their own aggressions, were never dispossessed of their town by actual conquest. Naturally, they were constantly in conflict with their neighbours, especially, with Telmessus and Pednelissus.[83] They had, however, the sense to conciliate Alexander when he passed through their country. In the war with Pednelissus, it would seem that, aided by the then most powerful chief of the neighbouring country, Achæus compelled the Selgians to sue for peace, to pay down 400 talents, to restore the prisoners they had taken, and to give 300 talents more. Yet, in an actual attack on the city he was repulsed with heavy loss (Polyb. v. 72-77). The coins of Selge prove its existence till a late date. One would have thought that such a place, would have left remains behind it amply sufficient for its identification; yet all we can say, certainly, of it is that it could not have been far to the east or south-east of Sagalassus. From Zosimus, we might be led to look for it *between* the Cestius and Eurymedon, for Tribigildus, having crossed the latter, found himself enclosed between it and the Melas: and possibly, Fellows did discover it. "On this promontory," says he, "stood one of the finest cities that probably ever existed, now presenting magnificent wrecks of grandeur. I rode for at least three miles through a part of the city, which was one pile of temples, theatres, and buildings, vieing with each other in splendour.... The material of the ruins, like those near Alaysóon (Sagalassus) had suffered much from exposure to the elements ... but the scale, the simple grandeur, and the beauty of style bespoke its date to be early Greek. The sculptured cornices frequently contain groups of figures fighting, wearing helmets and body armour, with shields and long spears." Unfortunately, Fellows did not find a single legible inscription, but the remains are, very likely, what Beaufort heard of at Alaya; viz., "extensive remains of an ancient Greek city with many temples, about fifteen hours' distance (say 35 miles) to the northward."[84] Lastly, we must give an account of the Pisidian, or more accurately, the Phrygian, Antioch, a town of the highest interest to the Christian reader, from its connection with St. Paul's early labours. It is remarkable that, 50 years ago, its position was not known, though the ancient notices of it, carefully studied, seem to point out, pretty clearly, where it ought to have been found. Little is known of this Antioch in early times, but it was, traditionally, a colony of Magnesia on the Mæander. Afterwards, like almost all the towns of Eastern and Central Asia Minor, it fell under the rule of the Seleucidæ, and, on their overthrow, was given by the Romans to Eumenes of Pergamus as one of the rewards for his faithful alliance. Subsequently, it was, for a while, under Amyntas the Lycaonian. At an early period of the empire, Antioch was known as Cæsarea, and somewhat later, according to Ulpian, its citizens enjoyed the Jus Italicum, that is, the same privileges as native Romans. At the time of St. Paul's visit it was the centre of a great commercial activity. According to Strabo, Antioch was on the south side of the mountain boundary of Phrygia and Pisidia (p. 577), Philomelium, a Phrygian town, being exactly to the north, the latter standing on level ground, while Antioch stood on a small eminence.[85] It was reserved for Mr. Arundell to show, almost certainly, its true site,[86] and his description is exceedingly interesting. Almost his first discovery was a "long and immense building, constructed with prodigious stones, and standing south and west." This was a church, not improbably constructed on the site of the Synagogue where St. Paul preached. "The remains of the aqueduct," he adds, "of which twenty-one arches are perfect, are the most splendid I ever beheld, the stones without cement, of the same massy dimensions as the wall."

> 83. It should be noted here, that the finding gold or silver coins at a place is not *alone* sufficient evidence for its name, though such a discovery is a presumption in favour of it. Where, however, a large number of small *copper* coins are found, the presumption becomes very strong. Obviously, gold and silver coins may, easily, pass from one site to another, simply as objects of commerce.

> 84. The neighbourhood of Selge produced, and produces, two useful botanical substances; one, the balsam of styrax or storax (liquid-amber orientalis), the juice of an umbrageous tree like the plane. Krinos (περὶ Στύρακος, Athens, 1862—) shows it has been correctly described by Aetius and Paulus Ægineta in the 6th and 7th centuries. It is noticed, also, in the Travels of the Russian Abbot of Tver, A.D. 1113-5. The author of the "Periplus" states that, in his time, storax went, as it does now, by way of the Red Sea to India. In India it is called Rose Malloes (Rosa Mallas, Rosum Alloes, Rosmal), perhaps from the Malay, Rasamala. This gum is extracted now by the Yuruk Turkomans, and is still used in the churches and mosques of S. Asia Minor for incense. One form of this substance is *Resina Benzoe—Gum Benjamin*, or *Benzoin* (Ibn Batuta's Travels, A.D. 1325-49—who says it comes from Java, and is called Java Frankincense or Camphor). The popular name is a corruption of *Lubán Jáwi* into *Ban-jawi*, &c. Crawfurd thinks it the old Malabathrum. It is stated by Vasco da Gama to be a product of Xarnuz (Siam).

> The other substance is *Rhizoma Iridis* (popularly Orris-root), used of old for giving a sweet odour to unguents (see Theophrastus, Dioskorides, and Pliny). The ancient arms of Florence were a white

lily or iris on a red shield. Orris-root was used as a perfume in England in 1480 (Wardrobe Accounts of Edward IV.), and, according to Gerarde, was grown here. In Tuscany it is still grown under the name of *Giaggiolo*.

85. All geographers, even Colonel Leake, seem to have gone astray here, in their interpretation of Strabo. Thus, D'Anville placed Antioch at Ak-Shehr (12 or 13 miles to the N., on the real site of Philomelium), and such, too, would seem to have been the opinion of the Latin historians of the Crusades, and even of Anna Comnena. In the Peutinger tables, a great road is marked from Iconium to Side, with a branch to Antioch. This is well explained, if the present *Yalobatch* represents Antioch.

86. We do not discredit Mr. Arundell's discovery, if we say that, in the actual text of his travels, he rather suggests a strong probability than proves his discovery. He did not find any inscription with the name of the town. His argument is, however, a strong inference that no other place in that neighbourhood, but Antioch, could have left such vast remains.

ANTIOCH OF PISIDIA.

A little further on he met with undoubted remains of a Temple of Bacchus, with the thyrsus or Bacchic emblem, and an inscription stating that one Calpurnius was "High Priest for life to the most glorious god BACCHUS." Another building, Mr. Arundell thinks, from the number of fluted columns, must have been a portico, "or the Temple of Lunus, or of Men Arcæus, whose worship was established at Antioch."[87] Le Quien, in his "Oriens Christianus," enumerated twenty-six bishops of Antioch. One of these, Methodius, and six other metropolitans subscribed the protest of the Eastern Church against the errors of Calvin. Hamilton, subsequently, found at Antioch an inscription reading ANTIOCHEAE CAESARE, which proves the truth of Arundell's inferences (i. p. 474).

> 87. Strabo speaks of the worship of this deity (ἱεροσύνη τις Μηνὸς Ἀρκαίου) at Antioch in olden times. It seems to have been abolished for some time, but to have been revived in Roman days, as coins exist with the god Lunus leaning on a column, and the legend COL. MEN. ANTIOCH, or MENSIS. COL. CAES. ANTIOCH.; and inscriptions exist with the name of L. Flavius Paulus—who is termed CVRATORI ARCÆ SANCTVARII. Strabo, a native of Amasia, states that a god called Men Pharnaces was worshipped at Cabira. From the coins we further learn, that the river at Antioch was called Antihos or Anthos, with ANTIOCH. COL., and the type of a woman reclining.

CILICIA had but few towns of much importance, and these chiefly on the coast or not far inland. Indeed, when we have mentioned Tarsus, Soli, Mallus, and Mopsuestia, we have noticed the principal places in this province. Of these, TARSUS[88] alone calls for any lengthened description. Of the early history of this city little is known, but a tradition, illustrated by one of its coins, asserted that Sardanapalus was buried there.[89] Its situation, however, led to its becoming the capital of Cilicia, a position it long retained. Tarsus stood on a rich and fertile plain on both sides of the river Cydnus. Historically, it is first noticed by Xenophon, as, in his day, a great and wealthy city, under a Persian satrap named Syennesis, the unwise ally of Cyrus the Younger. It remained under the Persian rule till the time of Alexander the Great, who nearly lost his life by imprudently bathing when too hot in the Cydnus (Curt. iii. 5; Arrian, ii. 4). In later days it was, generally, under the Seleucidæ, though, for a brief period, subject to the second and third Ptolemy.

> 88. We can see no reason for supposing Tarsus the "Tarshish" of the Bible. It did not export the kind of produce entrusted to the "ships of Tarshish," while the notices of it in the Bible (Gen. x. 4; 1 Chron. i. 7; Psalm lxxiv.; Isaiah lxvi. 19), imply a town or territory in the far west, whence, only, some of these products (as tin), so far as we know, were then obtainable. Hence we find the Phœnicians sailing thither in "long

ships" (Ezek. xxvii. 12, xxviii. 13; Jerem. x. 9); while the Roman writers, as Ovid (Met. xiv. 416), Silius Italicus (iii. 399), and Claudian (Epist. iii. v. 14), evidently use the name Tartessus as synonymous with "West." On the whole, it is most likely that Tartessus in Spain (considered loosely as a district rather than as a town) represents the Biblical Tarshish, and that "ships of Tarshish" is a term equivalent with "Indiamen."

89. A fine specimen of this coin (one of Antiochus VIII., king of Syria) was in the cabinet of the late General C. R. Fox. It was found, in 1848, in a leaden box, between Adana and Tarsus, some twenty feet under the surface of the ground. It has been engraved by Mr. Vaux, in his "Nineveh and Persepolis," 4th ed. 1856, p. 62. As its type—the so-called tomb of Sardanapalus—is found on other coins of Tarsus, as late as the time of Gordian, it is certain this myth maintained its hold on the popular mind for a long period. The story of the pageant of Cleopatra (Plut. Vit. Antonii) shows that the Cydnus must, in those days, have been navigable up to Tarsus, some eight or nine miles from the sea.

Supporting the cause of Cæsar, the great Julius himself paid Tarsus a visit, when the Tarsians changed the name of their city to Juliopolis. Augustus made it a "libera civitas." Hence, St. Paul, her most illustrious son, spoke truly, when he said it was "no mean city," and urged with equal truth and justice that he was "free-born," while his judge had only obtained this right "at a great price." The fact is, its position on the immediate confines of Syria and of Mesopotamia was of the highest importance to the Romans in their conflict with the Parthians and Persians. It still retains its old name, slightly modified into Tarsous, and is still the chief city of this part of Karamania.

Tarsus[90] was famous in early days for a remarkable class of coins, known as Satrap-money. Among these are coins of Tiribazus, Pharnabazus, Syennesis, and of other rulers, between B.C. 410 and B.C. 370. A description of a coin of Pharnabazus will show their general character. On the obverse of this silver piece is a bearded and helmeted head, possibly the mythological type of Bellerophon or Perseus, either of which would be appropriate to the Græco-Asiatic population of Cilicia, and the name of Pharnabazus in Phœnician letters. On the reverse, is a seated representation of the Jupiter of Tarsus, with the legend, *Baal-Tarz*, evidently the *Zeus Tersios* of the Greeks, recorded on another coin as ΔΙΟΣ ΤΑΡΣΕΩΝ, "Of the Jupiter of the Tarsians." The Duc de Luynes attributed this coin to the famous Pharnabazus (B.C. 413-374), who, originally Satrap of the N.W. district of Asia Minor, is memorable for the steady resistance he made to the Greeks, while the ruler of Lydia, Tissaphernes, on the other hand, accepted Lacedæmonian gold. If so, this coin must have been struck when

Pharnabazus had given (B.C. 397, 8) the command of the Persian fleet to the Athenian Conon, as Tarsus was then the centre of the operations against Cyprus. Another extremely rare coin of Pharnabazus, with his name in Greek, was struck at Lampsacus in Mysia, perhaps, for the payment of the Greek mercenaries of Artaxerxes.

> 90. Strabo has noted the studious habits of the Tarsians; no other city, not even Athens and Alexandria, surpassing it in the number and character of its schools. He adds, moreover, that the learned seldom remained in the city, but, like St. Paul, migrated elsewhere to complete their studies.

The towns along the coast of Cilicia have been very carefully studied by Captain Beaufort, who has identified many of them. The first of these, passing from W. to E., was CORACESIUM, a place historically interesting as having been held for a long time by Diodotus Tryphon, who, having revolted from Antiochus, set the first example of active defiance to the Seleucidæ; Coracesium was, also, the last place where the pirates made a united resistance to the forces of Pompey.[91] The whole story of these freebooters is very interesting. It is clear that their successes were mainly due to two things; first, the peculiar fitness of their ports along the seashore of Cilicia for prolonged resistance, with the high range of Taurus to fall back on if over-pressed; and, secondly, to the internecine squabbles of the kings of Cyprus, Egypt, and Syria with themselves and with the Romans, which made it, from time to time, the interest of each party to wink at their worst deeds. The Sacred Island of Delos was their chief western entrepôt; the increasing luxury of the Romans at the same time giving ample encouragement to their traffic in slaves.

> 91. *Anchiale*, which Colonel Leake thought the fort of Tarsus, like that city, claimed Sardanapalus as its founder. The legend was that Sardanapalus, the son of Anakyndaraxes, erected, in one day, the cities of Anchiale and Tarsus. No one, nowadays, accepts the verses given by Strabo, relating to this Sardanapalus and his deeds, as genuine, and Aristotle says the sentiments in them are fitter for the grave of an ox than for the tomb of a king (Cic. Tusc. Disput. v. 35). An early writer, Amyntas, records what recent research has shown to be probably the truth, viz. that Sardanapalus was buried at Nineveh.

The promontory of Alaya, identified by Captain Beaufort with Coracesium, rises, he says, abruptly "from a low, sandy isthmus which is separated from the mountains by a broad plain; two of its sides are cliffs of great height, and absolutely perpendicular, indeed the eastern side, on which the town is placed, is so steep that the houses seem to rest on each other." Other places along this coast eastwards are, LAERTES (the birthplace of Diogenes

Laertius), ἐπὶ λόφου μαστοειδοῦς, "on a hill, in form like a woman's breast," and SELINUS, a river and a town (now Selinty), the first of which is mentioned by Strabo, and the second by Livy. Its later name of Trajanopolis it owed to the sudden death there of the Emperor Trajan (A.D. 117), but, at a later period, the old name was revived in connection with an episcopal church (Hierocles). Beaufort speaks of its magnificent cliffs—"On the highest point of these," he says, "are the ruins of a castle which commands the ascent of the hill in every direction, and looks perpendicularly down on the sea." He notices also several other large structures, and, among these, a mausoleum (perhaps that of Trajan), an agora, a theatre, and an aqueduct. The supposed mausoleum, 70 feet long and 50 feet wide, is constructed of large well-cut blocks of stone and contains only one vault. Cyprus, distant sixty-five miles, can be clearly seen from this headland.

The next important seaport was ANEMURIUM (now *Anamur*), in the neighbourhood of which Beaufort discovered a perfect city of tombs. "These tombs," says he, "are small buildings detached from each other and mostly of the same size, though varying in their proportions; the roofs are arched, and the exterior of the walls is dashed with a composition of plaster and small particles of burnt red brick. Each tomb consists of two chambers: the inner one is subdivided into cells or receptacles for the bodies, and the outer apartment is supplied with small recesses and shelves, as if for the purpose of depositing the funereal offerings, or the urns that contained the ashes. The castle strongly resembles some of the ancient castles of Great Britain. Its keep or citadel is placed on a small rocky eminence, and commands two open courts.... The extreme dimensions are about 800 feet by 300 feet."

CELENDERIS (now *Chelindreh*) was noted in ancient history as the place which Piso, the enemy of Germanicus, attempted to take (Tacit. An. xi. 80), and appears, also, in the Ecclesiastical annals, as one of the episcopal towns of Isauria. As the nearest point of communication with Cyprus, it is still occupied by a small population. There are some remains of a fortress which Tacitus describes as of great strength; while many arched vaults, sepulchres and sarkophagi may be seen on the spot. All along this part of the coast of Cilicia the presence of the Crusaders is clearly shown in the names of existing places, as, for instance, in *Cavalière* and *Provençal Island*; indeed, Vertot records that, during the settlement of the Christian knights at Rhodes, they took possession of several islands and castles along the shores of Asia Minor. Another place, some eight or nine miles inland, SELEFKEH, the ancient SELEUCEIA AD CALYCADNUM, is also specially noticed by De Jauna in his History of Armenia, as given by the king of Armenia to the knights of Rhodes for their services. This town, which owed its real or supposed origin to Seleukus Nicator, was famous for its schools of literature and philosophy: Athenæus and Xenarchus, two well-known Peripatetics, having been born there. Seleucia was still in existence in the time of Ammianus, and the ecclesiastical historians, Socrates and Sozomen, speak of Councils having been held here.

Beaufort reports the existence at Selefkeh of many ruins on the west side of the river, and, especially, of an enormous reservoir lined with hard cement (the *"opus Signinum"* or *"Coccio pesto"* of the Roman aqueducts). This structure is 150 feet long by 75 feet broad and 35 feet deep, and could, therefore, have held nearly 10,000 tons of water. A little further on is a place called *Korghoz*, possibly, the CORYCUS of antiquity, and the site of the Corycian cave, in mythology, the fabled abode of the giant, Typhôs;[92] but, more probably, the crater of an extinct volcano. Strabo says it was a deep and broad circular valley, the lower part rugged, but covered with shrubs and evergreens, and, especially, with saffron, which was abundant here. From an internal cavity gushed forth a copious stream, which, for a while lost, after a brief course, reappeared near the sea, which it joined. This was called the "bitter water." Beaufort found two places bearing the name of Korgho Kalaler (castles), there being many signs in the neighbourhood of the former existence of a city of considerable size:—"A mole of great unhewn rocks projects at one angle from the fortress about 100 yards across the bay, terminated by a solid building twenty feet square."[93] Can this be the remains of an ancient *pharos* or lighthouse? We should add that the places, hitherto described, belong to what was usually called Cilicia Tracheia; those we shall now notice, belonging, on the other hand, to the plain country.

92. Pind. Pyth. i. 31, thus speaks of him and of his home:—

Τυφὼς ἑκατὸν κάρανος· τὸν ποτὲ

Κιλίκιον θρέψεν πολυώνυμον

ἄντρον.

He is also called, Pyth. viii. 26,

Τυφὼς Κίλιξ ἑκατόγκρανος.

Æschylus, too, gives him the same epithet of "hundred-headed."—Prom. Vinct. 350.

93. Pomponius Mela (i. 13) gives an even fuller description of this famous cave, probably from the same original author, Callisthenes.

Of these we take first, SOLI, a colony (Strabo tells us) from Lindus, a relationship the Solians did not forget during subsequent negotiations with the Romans. Soli is first mentioned in Xenophon's Anabasis, and must, in the following seventy years, have rapidly increased, as Alexander the Great fined the people 200 talents for their attachment to the Persian empire. After having been destroyed by Tigranes, Pompey placed there some of the Cilician pirates whom he had spared; at the same time changing the name of the city to Pompeiopolis. Most of the existing remains are, therefore, Roman. "The first object," says Beaufort, "which presented itself on landing was a beautiful harbour or basin, with parallel sides and circular ends; it is entirely artificial, being formed by surrounding moles or walls fifty feet in thickness and seven feet in height.... Opposite to the entrance of the harbour a portico rises from the surrounding quay, and opens to a double row of two hundred columns which, crossing the town, communicates with the principal gate towards the country; and from the outside of that gate a paved road continues, in the same line, to a bridge over a small river.... Even in its present state of wreck, the effect of the whole is so imposing, that the most illiterate seaman in the ship could not behold it without emotion." The actual execution of these columns is, however, poor; and, of the original two hundred, only forty-four are now standing.[94] Soli was the birthplace of Chrysippus, Philemon, and Aratus.

> 94. It has been said that the term σολοικσμος—*solæcismus*—*solecism*—meaning ungrammatical speech—was derived from the people of Soli; but this accusation is not certain (Cf. Strab. xiv. 671; Eustath. ad Dion. Perieg. v. 875; Suidas in voce Σόλοι). There was another Soli in Cyprus, the inhabitants of which were usually termed Solii (Σόλιοι), to distinguish them from those on the mainland, who were termed Σολεῖς. Both, probably, spoke but indifferent Greek.

ADANA, which is noticed first in the Mithradatic War, by Appian, and, subsequently, by Pliny, Ptolemy, Dio Cassius, Procopius, and the Byzantine historians, like Tarsus, adopted the name of Hadrian. It is still a place of some size, and the capital of the Pashalik of the same name.

Near the mouth of the river *Pyramus* (now *Gihoon*), and further up, are three towns which may be taken together. The first is MALLUS, very near the sea, on the left bank of the river over which Alexander threw a bridge, in Mallotis, Strabo's name for the circumjacent district; or Megarsus (possibly an earlier name for Mallus,) described in Lycophon as standing on a "sea-worn hill"—an expression Beaufort says accurately applies to a place now called *Karadash*.[95] Mallus retained its name, slightly modified to Malo, till mediæval times (Sanut. Secret. Fid. li. p. iv. c. 26): 2ndly, above Mallus, MOPSUESTIA, the creation of a certain mythical hero called Mopsus. According to Pliny, this town was a "free" city, and Procopius states that Justinian repaired the bridge over it (Ædif. v. 5). During the Byzantine period the name was modified to *Mensis*. Still further up the same river was ANAZARBA (sometimes called *Cæsarea ad Anazarbum*), the capital, in the fifth century, of Eastern Cilicia as Tarsus was of the Western—(Hierocles). It was nearly destroyed by earthquakes in the reigns of Justin and Justinian (Procop. Hist. Arcana, c. 18; Cedren., p. 299). Dioskorides and Oppian were born there. The last place in Cilicia to which we shall call attention is ISSUS, ever memorable as the scene of the famous conflict between Alexander and Darius. Its modern name, Scandaroon or Alexandretta, is obviously derived from Alexandreia. The town stood at the foot of the main chain of Mount Amanus, and, at the head of the gulf to which it gave its name. It was early (as might have been expected from its position) a considerable town, but, in Strabo's time, had ceased to be more than a small port. Cicero, in his expedition against the mountaineers in the neighbourhood stayed there for some time (Epist. ad Attic. v. 20). The famous defile leading from Cilicia into Syria was to the east of the town.

95. Lycophron's words are—

Πυράμου πρὸς ἐκβολαῖς.

Αἰπὺς δ' ἁλιβρὸς ὄχμος ἐν μεταιχμίῳ
Μέγαρσος.—(Cassandr. v. 439.)

The river Pyramus, according to Scylax, could be ascended by ships as far as Mallus, but the poets feigned that its mud would, in time, join Cyprus to the mainland. The poetical words are—

Ἔσσεται ἐσσομένοις ὅτε Πύραμος εὐρυοδίνης
Ἠϊόνα προχέων ἱερὴν εἰς Κύπρον ἵκεται.

It has been disputed whether Megarsus was really on the river, but the legend on its coins—ΜΕΓΑΡΣΕΩΝ ΠΡΟΣ ΤΩ ΠΥΡΑΜΩ—sets *this* question at rest. The Aleian plain, which lay between Tarsus and Mallus, was the traditional scene of Bellerophon's disaster (Il. z. 200).

CHAPTER IV.

Isaura—Iconium—Lystra—Derbe—Apamea Cibotus—Aezani—Synnada—Philomelium—Laodicea Combusta—Hierapolis—Laodicea ad Lycum—Colossæ—Ancyra—Pessinus—Tavium—Nazianzus—Cæsarea ad Argæum—Tyana—Comana—Trapezus—Amastris—Sinope—Prusa ad Olympum—Nicæa—Nicomedia—Islands of Greece—Lesbos—Samos—Chios—Rhodus—Messrs. Biliotti and Saltzmann—Cyprus—Mr. Lang—General Palma di Cesnola.

HAVING now spoken of some of the principal places in the west and south of Asia Minor, it will, we think, be convenient to take next those towards its centre, in *Cappadocia*, *Phrygia*, and *Galatia*. We must, however, notice, first, the two small districts of *Lycaonia* and *Isauria*, which are really portions cut out of the larger adjoining provinces. Isauria will not detain us long, as there is little in it that can be called Greek. It was, as it has ever been, a wild mountain district, with a population unsubdued till about the time of Constantine; and, even after that, if the Byzantine writers are worthy of credit, whole armies of Constantinopolitan Greeks melted as snow in conflict with these robber tribes. Ancient authors knew little of Isauria except its northern part, all to the south, with its capital, ISAURA, being to them, practically, a *terra incognita*. As marauders, however, the Isaurians were so troublesome to their neighbours, that the Roman Senate sent a considerable force against them, in B.C. 73, under P. Servilius, whose success won for him the title of "Isauricus." This conquest, however, so to call it, was but temporary, and, not long after, Amyntas of Lycaonia lost his life in an attempt to crush one of their tribes. In later days, one of their chieftains, Trebellianus, claimed for himself the rank of Emperor, and struck coins; and the Isaurians boasted, also, of one genuine Emperor, Zeno Isauricus, A.D. 474-491.

Of its chief town, ISAURA, we have coins of the time of Geta and Elagabalus bearing the title of ΜΗΤΡΟΠΟΛΕΩΣ ΙΣΑΥΡΩΝ. Mr. Hamilton has satisfactorily identified its site on the line of road between Iconium and Anemurium—a determination in agreement with Pliny's statement (v. 27), that the province of Isauria stretched to the sea in that direction: he adds that the tradition of their ancient robber propensities is still remembered by the existing peasantry of the district, though, considering what this country has undergone during the last fifteen hundred years, any such tradition is not worth much. Mr. Hamilton found the ruins of the capital on one of the loftiest ridges between the Taurus and the plains of Konieh (Iconium) at an elevation of quite 5,000 feet above the sea, the wild and inaccessible district around it offering, as he observes, "little or no temptation to the rapacity of its neighbours." An inscription found on the spot fully confirmed his previous surmises: it was on a triumphal arch, in honour of the Emperor

Hadrian, and, on the ground near it, was a marble globe, a common emblem of Imperial power "I afterwards," says he, "found several other inscriptions in this part of the town; of these, No. 432, lying near the *agora*, is full of interest, as alluding to several buildings formerly erected in its neighbourhood." Strabo had remarked (xii. p. 569) that Amyntas died before he had completed the town wall, and this Hamilton found to be literally true, everything around indicating a town entirely rebuilt, the wall itself, its octagonal towers, temples, and triumphal arches being constructed in the same peculiar style. "There is," says he, "an air of newness in its very ruins, as if it had been destroyed before it was half built, although it must not be forgotten that it flourished for many centuries after the death of Augustus."

In Lycaonia there were few towns of importance, except ICONIUM, LAODICEA, DERBE, and LYSTRA, the geological features of the country being unfavourable to the existence of a large population. Travellers who have seen both compare Lycaonia with the interior of Australia. Both were, by nature, extensive sheep-walks (thus, Amyntas had as many as 300 flocks of sheep); while both, alike, had much of arid and salt desert, fitted only for camels. The central plain of Lycaonia, from Kiepert's map, seems the largest in Asia Minor, and resembles the *steppes* of Central Asia and of southern Russia. Ainsworth tells how his camels browsed off the tops of the *Mesembryanthemum* and *Salicornia*, reminding them, as these, doubtless, did, of plains more familiar to them than those of Asia Minor. Strabo made Isauria part of Lycaonia.

The principal town of Lycaonia, ICONIUM, is mentioned first by Xenophon, who considered it the most eastern one of Phrygia, at one day's journey, according to Cicero, from Philomelium (Ak-shehr). Its position, amid many small streams, which exhaust themselves in watering its gardens, and as the meeting-place of several of the most important of the Roman roads through Asia Minor, made it, from the first, an important *entrepôt*; and, though Strabo calls it πολίχνιον (a little town), the account of Pliny, and the narrative in the Acts of the Apostles, prove it was a large and populous place in the middle of the first century A.D. Indeed, in Pliny's time, its territory embraced fourteen towns, stretched around the capital (v. 27). Cicero was there for several days previously to his Cilician campaign. Iconium will always be invested with much interest owing to St. Paul's visits to it; the first of which was immediately after his expulsion from Antioch in Pisidia, when the Apostles "shook off the dust of their feet." Messrs. Conybeare and Howson have well remarked, that the vast plain and the distant mountains are the most interesting features of modern *Konieh*; for these, probably, remain as they were in the first century of Christianity, while the town has been repeatedly destroyed and rebuilt. Little, indeed, remains of Greek or Roman

Iconium, except the inscriptions and fragments of sculptures built into the Turkish walls.

Iconium was famous in the early Middle Ages as the capital of the Seljuk Sultans,[96] but was taken by the Emperor Barbarossa, during the second Crusade, in his famous but futile attempt to force his way through Asia Minor. To quote the picturesque words of Gibbon, "Forty campaigns in Germany and Italy had taught Barbarossa to command; and his soldiers, even the princes of the empire, were accustomed under his reign to obey. As soon as he had lost sight of Philadelphia and Laodicea, the last cities of the Greek frontier, he plunged into the salt and barren desert, a land (says the historian) of horror and tribulation. During twenty days every step of his fainting and sickly march was besieged by innumerable hordes of Turkmans, whose numbers and fury seemed after each defeat to multiply and to inflame. The emperor continued to struggle and to suffer; and such was the measure of his calamities, that when he reached the gates of Iconium no more than 1,000 knights were able to serve on horseback. By a sudden and resolute assault he defeated the guards and stormed the capital of the sultan, who sued for pardon and peace. The road was now open, and Frederic advanced in a career of triumph, till he was unfortunately drowned in a petty torrent of Cilicia."[97] Leake points out that its walls, still between two or three miles round, are full of inscriptions and of other ancient remains, which the Seljuks seem to have tried to preserve.

> 96. The Seljuks had first been at Nicæa; but, when the Crusaders took that town, in A.D. 1099, they fell back on Iconium, which they held, with the exception of the brief interval of its capture by Barbarossa in 1189, till the irruption of the Mongols, under Jinghis Khán, and of his grandson, Huláku, who broke down their power completely. Konieh has been an integral part of the Turkish empire ever since the days of Bayazíd.
>
> 97. There has been much doubt in which "Cilician torrent" Barbarossa was drowned. The name in the record is the "Saleph," which maybe a corruption of Selefkeh (Seleucia), a name sometimes given to the Calycadnus, as a chief town on it. There seems no reason for drowning him in the Cydnus, or modern Kara-su.

The position of LYSTRA and DERBE are still uncertain. Of Derbe, we know that it was the residence of a robber chief of Lycaonia, named Antipater,[98] who was ultimately subdued by Amyntas (Strabo, xii. p. 569), while Strabo and Stephanus Byzantinus placed it on the borders of Isauria towards Cappadocia. St. Luke, however, and Hierocles placed it as clearly in Lycaonia. If Lystra and Derbe stood in St. Luke's order, Lystra would be the nearest to Iconium; but, though mentioned in Pliny and Ptolemy, we have no further hint as to its actual position. One of its bishops was present at the Council of Chalcedon. The interesting account in the Acts xiv. 6-21, of the behaviour of the people of Lystra, when St. Paul proved his Divine mission by the cure of the cripple, must be fresh in the mind of every one. With regard to the speculative identifications of the sites of Lystra and Derbe, it is, perhaps, worth stating that S.E. of Konieh is a remarkable isolated hill, the Karadagh or Black mountain. Not far from this mountain, Leake and Hamilton placed these two towns, the former twenty miles S.E. of Iconium, the latter at some remarkable ruins around its base, called by the Turks Bin-bir-kalis-seh, or the 1,001 churches. Mr. Hamilton and Mr. Edward Falkener have both examined this remarkable group of ruined churches, recording, as they clearly do, some site peculiarly revered in early Christian times. Mr. Falkener's remarks on these curious monuments are much to the point. "The principal group," says he, "of the Bin-bir-Kalisseh, lies at the foot of Karadagh.... Perceiving ruins on the slope of the mountain, I began to ascend, and, on reaching them, perceived that they were churches, and, looking upwards, descried others yet above me, and climbing from one to the other, I at length gained the summit, where I found two churches. On looking down, I perceived churches on all sides of the mountain scattered about in various positions.... There are about two dozen in tolerable preservation, and the remains of perhaps forty may be traced altogether.... The mountain must have been considered sacred; all the ruins are of the Christian epoch, and, with the exception of a huge palace, every building is a church." It appears from the Acts that, besides the Greek, there was still extant a local Lycaonian dialect, and this is what we should expect from what we know in the cases of Caria, Lycia, and Phrygia, respectively. There are, however, no certain means, now, of determining what was its character, and whether it was of Semitic or of Indo-European descent.

> 98. Cicero (ad Fam. xiii. 73) says he was treated with much civility by the Lycaonian Antipater—a view of things not agreeable to his correspondent Q. Philippus, who had been previously proconsul of Asia Minor. Stephanus Byzantinus states that Derbe was sometimes called "Delbia," a word in the Lycaonian dialect said to mean "juniper." It is possible that two words of much similarity have been confounded in the MSS., viz. λιμήν, a harbour or port, and λίμνη, a lake or marsh; and that the town was really on the shores of one of the many internal lakes of that part of Asia Minor. The position of Derbe near the lake of *Ak Ghieul*, and its resemblance to Delbia, with the modern name of *Divleh*, as suggested by Hamilton, tends to its identification with Divleh.

Having dealt pretty fully with the provinces and towns of Asia Minor to the west and south, with some notice of those in Lycaonia, we propose now to notice the chief ones in *Phrygia* and *Galatia*, though we have not space to weigh nicely the limits of each of these districts, which were, indeed, till Roman times, in a state of constant change. Rome, as we know, thought fit to include under the name of Asia more than one piece arbitrarily cut out of the older provinces; Roman Asia being to the rest of Asia Minor much what Portugal on maps was to Spain.

The Phrygians themselves were, like the Mysians, probably of Thracian origin, as the name Bryges, or Briges, is found in Macedonia, and is, probably, connected with the Celtic word "briga," as in Artobriga. We find also in the neighbouring province of Bithynia a tribe called Bebryces. The Phrygians have also been supposed to have some connection with Armenia—a theory, however, mainly resting on their legend of a primeval flood, and of the resting of an ark on the mountains near Celænæ.

It is certain that the people of this part of Asia Minor were very much intermixed. Thus, the Trojans and Mysians were almost certainly members of the great Phrygian race; for Hecuba was a Phrygian princess, and Hector a common Phrygian name. One stream of immigrators may, therefore, have come from Armenia into Europe, and have, thence, returned somewhat later to Phrygia, the Phrygians, like the Macedonians, being said to be unable to pronounce the φ (ph), and saying Bilippus and Berenice, for Philippus and Pherenice: in the army, too, of Xerxes, the Armenians and Phrygians wear similar armour. Recent researches by Baron Texier and Mr. Hamilton have shown that the Phrygians had a peculiar style of architecture, the former having discovered an entire town carved out of the solid rock. Tombs, too, occur, in construction resembling the lion gate of Mycenæ; while there is also a legend of a Phrygian Pelops in Argolis. Phrygian religious rites were widely accepted by remote districts of the ancient world, the goddess Cybele being strictly a Phrygian deity, and the wild "orgies" of her worship essentially Asiatic.

Of the towns of Phrygia we take first APAMEA, as unquestionably one of the most important for its varied history and for the many persons of note who are linked with it. Its foundation is due to Antiochus Soter, who named it after his mother Apama. According to Strabo, it stood at the source of the river Marsyas, which burst forth in the middle of the city, and flowed thence into the Mæander; and, though this description is not quite borne out by recent observations, the identity of its size with the modern village of Deenare or Denair, has been satisfactorily shown by an inscription found by Mr. Arundell, reading—QUI. APAMEAE. NEGOCIANTVR. H. C. (hoc. curaverunt). "The merchants frequenting Apamea have taken care (to erect this monument)."[99] Cicero, who was appointed proconsul of Cilicia in B.C. 51, has left us many interesting particulars about it in his letters to his friends, as he was much there. At this place, too, he deposited one of the three copies of his quæstor's accounts, at the same time refusing to accept for himself or to permit his soldiers to appropriate, any of the booty taken from the enemy. In a letter to Can. Sallustius, proquæstor, he adds: "I shall leave the money at Laodicea ... in order to avoid the hazard, both to self and the commonwealth, of conveying it in specie." While governing his province, one of his friends requested him to procure some panthers for him. This he did, and at his own expense, remarking at the same time "that the beasts made sad complaints against him, and resolved to quit the country, since no snares were laid in his province for any other creatures but themselves."[100]

> 99. Arundell (i. p. 192). He remarks further: "Apamea may now be asserted to have been at *Deenare* with as much confidence as that Ephesus or Sardis stood on the sites which still preserve their names. Apamea stood, we should add, nearly, though not quite, on the site of the ancient Celænæ. It suffered so severely from earthquakes, that the Roman tribute due from it was remitted, A.D. 53, for five years (Tacit. Ann. xii. 58)."

> 100. Mr. Arundell remarks the panthers are still (1834) occasionally found in the neighbourhood of Smyrna.

COIN OF APAMEA CIBOTUS.

But, besides the classical history of Apamea, which is well enough known, this place was accredited with a tradition referring to the Ark, which, though purely legendary, cannot be omitted here; the more so as the story of the Ark resting after the Flood on one of the heights near Apamea has been supposed by some to have given that city the title of "Cibotus," or "Apamea of the

Chest."[101] Indeed, Mount Ararat was placed by some on the confines of Phrygia. The coin of Alexander Severus, of which we give a copy above, is supposed to refer to this story. On the reverse is the name of the people of Apamea, and, above, a square structure resting on a rock, and surrounded by water. In this box are two figures, male and female, and in front the word NΩE (Noe). It is, therefore, a fair presumption that the maker of the medal did mean to represent Noah and wife. Two other persons, also a man and a woman, stand in front of the supposed ark. If, as we believe, the Scriptural deluge took place in Babylonia, some features of its story might easily have found their way to Phrygia; while, independently of this, we know that, even in the days of St. Paul, there were Jewish synagogues in many of the great towns of Asia Minor. Moreover, during the 150 years between St. Paul and Alexander Severus, some, at least, of the more striking events recorded in the Bible must have become popularly known.

> 101. It ought to be added that the ancient name of Apamea, when the capital of Phrygia, was Celænæ, and that, in Roman times, though Laodicea Combusta was the residence of the proconsul, it was considered, commercially, inferior only to Ephesus. Laodicea was one of the towns privileged to strike those curious silver coins known by the name of *Cistophori*. Though we do not accept the Ark story as the origin of this name "Kibotus," we cannot say that we attach much, if any, weight to many other derivations that have been proposed.

The next place we notice is AZANI, or AEZANI (for both spellings occur), the latter, that of the coins of the place, being the more preferable. It is certain that the present Lord Ashburnham, in 1824, was the first to determine where it stood, though this discovery has, with some carelessness, been often attributed wrongly. It is now called Tchandur Hissar, and, from Keppel, Hamilton, and Fellows, appears to possess some ruins of remarkable beauty, and more than one Roman bridge. Hamilton (i. 101) states that its Ionic temple (of which Fellows and Pullan give drawings) is one of the most perfect in Asia Minor. Rather curiously, no walls have been found; but the place has suffered from plunderers severely, every tomb having been despoiled.

In *Phrygia Magna*, as distinguished from *Phrygia Epictetus*, a place of early notice and of long importance was SYNNADA, which we hear of first in connection with the famous march of Cn. Manlius against the Gallo-Græci. Cicero visited it in his progress towards Cilicia. In Pliny's time, it was the judicial centre of the neighbourhood. It was chiefly famous for a beautiful marble with purple spots and veins, to which Statius alludes (Silv. i. 5, 56). Texier was the first to discover the actual quarries, which were, as the natives of old asserted, not at Synnada, but at Docimia; whence the marble itself was sometimes called "Docimites lapis." Paulus Silentiarius, in a poem on the church of St. Sophia, has well described its character. Docimia itself was probably at the end of the plain where Synnada was itself situate. Hierocles makes Synnada a bishopric of Phrygia Salutaris. Its ruins are now called *Eski Kara Hissar.*

On the main road from Synnada towards Iconium stood PHILOMELIUM, the "city of nightingales," now, since the discovery of the true site of the Pisidian Antioch, identified with Ak-shehr. It was a place of much value to the early Turkish rulers, and many handsome Saracenic buildings may still be seen; hence, too, it is often mentioned in the wars between the Greek emperors and the Sultans of Iconium, as in Procopius (Hist. Arc. 18) and Anna Comnena (p. 473).[102]

> 102. PHILOMELIUM, now called *Afium Kara Hissar* (the "black castle of opium"), has much interest as the centre of the great Asia-Minor trade in that drug, the medicinal properties of which were known to Theophrastus in the third century B.C., under the name of μηκώνιον. Scribonius Largus (A.D. 40), also, knew that the best form of it was procured from the capsules, and not from the leaves of the poppy (Berthold, Argent. 1786, c. iii. s. 2). Dioscorides, thirty years later, calls the juice of these capsules ὀπός (Angl. *Sap*), and the cutting them ὀπίζειν. Hence, the name, *Opium.* Pliny (iv. c. 65, xx. c. 76) points out the medicinal use of "Opion," and Celsus calls the extracted juice "*Lacryma papaveris.*" Obviously, from this "Opion" comes the Arabic "Afyum," which is found in many Eastern languages, and may have been spread all the more, owing to Muhammad's interdiction of the use of wine. In India, *Opium* is noticed, first, in Barbosa's Travels, A.D. 1511 (ap. Hakluyt), who found it, at that time, in Malabar and Calicut. Neither Chinese nor Sanskrit has a native word for this drug. *Opium Thebaicum* is mentioned as early as A.D. 1288-96, by Simon Januensis, Physician to Pope Nicholas IV. (Clavis Sanationis. Venet. 1510); and Kæmpfer (1687) remarks that compounds of opium, nutmegs, &c., were largely sold in his time, as long before, under the name of *"Theriaka."*

But the most important place in the neighbourhood was LAODICEA, often called "Combusta," "the burnt," which is to be carefully distinguished from the other town of the same name we shall presently describe in connection with Hierapolis, and which is generally called "ad Lycum," "on the Lycus," in the province of Lydia. Recent geographers, however, give both these towns to Phrygia. Laodicea Combusta was about nine hours N.W. of Iconium, and under its modern names of Yorgan Ladik or Ladik-el-Tchaus, is famous throughout Asia Minor for its manufacture of carpets. It has been, popularly, supposed, that it derived its name from the existence at it of some remarkable volcanic agencies. This, however, Mr. Hamilton has clearly shown, is not the case. "There is not," he says, "a particle of volcanic or igneous rock in the neighbourhood; the hills consist of blue marble, and of the argillaceous and micaceous schists with which that rock is usually associated." He thinks it may, at some time or other, have been burnt down, and, on being rebuilt, have received this distinguishing title. The inscriptions he found there, though in great abundance, have little interest, being chiefly funereal: they are all carved out of the dark blue-veined limestone of the adjoining hills.

The last three places in Phrygia, which we think it necessary to note especially, we shall take together, as situate near one another, and, historically, closely connected. These cities are HIERAPOLIS, LAODICEA, (ad Lycum), and COLOSSÆ.

HIERAPOLIS is chiefly remarkable for waters so loaded with petrifying materials as to have completely changed, by their deposits, the face of the country in the course of centuries; a result, noticed by many ancient authors, as Vitruvius, Pausanias, &c. Chandler states that a cliff near the town is one entire incrustation, and describes its appearance as that of "an immense frozen cascade, the surface wavy, as of water at once fixed, or in its headlong course suddenly petrified."[103] An excellent view of this curious scene is given in Mr. Davis's "Anatolica," p. 100. Besides its remarkable petrifying power, Strabo states also that the waters of Hierapolis were famous for dyeing; and it is curious confirmation of this statement, that an early English traveller (Dr. Smith, in 1671) copied an inscription referring to a "*company of dyers*" (ἡ ἐργασία τῶν βαφέων). The position of Hierapolis must have been very imposing, placed as it was on a high piece of ground, "200 paces wide, and a mile in length." Abundant ruins still remain, consisting of the relics of three Christian churches, one 300 feet long, and of a gymnasium, considered by Leake to be one of the only three "which are in a state of preservation sufficient to give any useful information on the subject of these buildings," together with a prodigious number of fallen columns, in the wildest state of confusion. It seems a pity that no efficient steps have been taken to excavate thoroughly such a site as that of Hierapolis, where monuments of much historical interest, possibly, too, of surpassing excellence as sculpture, might reasonably be anticipated. Hierapolis is specially noticed in St. Paul's epistle to the Colossians (iv. 13), which shows clearly that, at that time, there were many converts to Christianity, probably owing to the zeal of Epaphras, who had been long a common labourer with the Apostle. Somewhat later, Hierapolis appears in Hierocles as the metropolis of Phrygia; and Arundell gives a list of the bishops of the see whose names have been preserved. The present ruins are called *Pambouk Kalessi*.

> 103. Mr. Hamilton says he could distinctly trace six different cascades, each of which had left a separate incrustation. The ancient

city itself was built on a terrace entirely formed by this or similar incrustations. He adds: "But if the appearance of the encrusted cliff was curious when seen from below, it became infinitely more so when we looked down upon it from the road, and the detail of its structure became more apparent. The wavy and undulating lines of solid matter which extend over the surface look as if a large river had been suddenly arrested in its course and converted into stone."

LAODICEA *"ad Lycum"* was, in the time of Strabo, one of the principal places in this province, and the centre of the Roman power in this part of Asia. Many men of great wealth, it is said, contributed to its early magnificence; Strabo noticing Hiero, who, besides greatly embellishing it during his lifetime, left to it by will the sum of 2,000 talents, together with the orator Zeno, and his son Polemo, who was made by Augustus king of part of Pontus. There are some difficulties in reconciling the statements of ancient authors about the rivers that flowed by or close to this town, and even recent investigations have not made this matter quite clear. Four rivers are mentioned in connection with it—the Lycus, Asopus, Caprus, and the Cadmus. Of these the first is, unquestionably, the most important, as having given its name to the town. It is likely these difficulties have been increased by the earthquakes noticed by Strabo, who says that Laodicea, more than any other town, was subject to their baneful influence. His words are remarkable (εἰ γάρ τις ἄλλη καὶ ἡ Λαοδίκεια εὔσειστος, Strab. p. 578). Such earthquakes would, naturally modify the course of these streams.[104] Col. Leake calls especial attention to the importance of a thorough investigation of the ruins of all these great towns: so much is still on the surface, that he thinks there is reasonable hope of the discovery of much still buried. The same, to a smaller extent, would, probably, prove true of other cities in the vale of the Mæander; for Strabo thought that Philadelphia, Sardes, and Magnesia ad Sipylum were not less than Laodicea, and had all alike suffered from the ravages of earthquakes; and this view was completely supported by Arundell from his own personal observations at Laodicea (Seven Churches, p. 85).

> 104. Compare what Tacitus says, Annal. ii. 79, xiv. 97, and Herodotus's statement that the Lycus disappeared at Colossæ, close by, a statement in some degree confirmed by Strabo (xii. 578), and other remarks bearing on the history of this important town in Polyb. v. 57, 3; Cic. Verr. i. 3; Epist. ad Fam. iii. 5, 7; Tacit. Annal. iv. 55; Philostr. p. 543.

Laodicea suffered severely at the hands of Mithradates, but, with the reign of Augustus, its real fame and prosperity arose and long continued. About A.D. 1097 it was seized by the Turks, and subsequently was, alternately, in their hands or in those of the Byzantine emperors. In 1190 the Emperor Barbarossa was welcomed by the then inhabitants with much kindness, but, shortly afterwards, it was wholly desolated by the Turks. The zeal of St. Paul for the Church of Laodicea suggests that there must early have been abundant converts to the new faith in its neighbourhood. It is, however, also clear that their allegiance was not very trustworthy, and that they were much inclined to accept a modified form of Christianity. St. Paul's words in his Epistle to the Colossians (ii. 1) show this plainly enough—"For I would," says he, "that ye knew what great conflict I have for you, and for them at Laodicea, and for as many as have not seen my face in the flesh." Again, "When this epistle is read among you, cause that it be read also in the Church of the Laodiceans" (iv. 16). The Book of Revelation contains, also, strong strictures on the lukewarmness of the Laodiceans. "I know thy works, that thou art neither cold nor hot; I would thou wert cold or hot. So then, because thou art lukewarm, and neither cold nor hot, I will spue thee out of my mouth" (Rev. iii. 15, 16). Laodicea, though sometimes called Ladik, is more usually known as Eski-Hissar, the Turkish form of the common Levantine title of Palæo-Castro—"Old Castle."

COLOSSÆ, the last of the three towns, has been much confused with the other two, from the haste and want of accurate observation of different travellers. Much time is, indeed, requisite for the comparison of the brief notes of ancient authors with the existing facts. It is not certain when Colossæ was founded, or to what circumstances it owes its name, but it existed some centuries before the Christian era, as it is mentioned by Herodotus as a large and flourishing town of Phrygia when Xerxes passed through it in B.C. 481, on his way from Cappadocia to Sardes (vii. 30); nor had it, apparently, at all decayed when visited by Cyrus the Younger, about eighty years subsequently, (Xen. Anab. i. 2). Like the people of the adjacent Laodicea, the Colossians were great growers of wool. It was nearly destroyed in the days of Nero, but it survived, at all events, as the name of a Christian bishopric, till the time of Hierocles's *Synecdemus*. Somewhat later, a new town named Chonas was built there, the certain identification of its ruins being mainly due to the fact that Nicetas the Annalist was born there. St. Paul, as we know, wrote an epistle to the Colossians, but his words, "Since we *heard* of your faith in Christ Jesus," seem to imply that he was never there himself. On the other hand, Epaphras, who was a native of Colossæ, and Onesimus, are specially noted as having preached there.

Colossæ has been repeatedly visited by travellers, such as Dr. Smith, Picenini, Pococke, and Arundell; but to Mr. Hamilton we owe the clearest notice of it, and the reconciling of many points not understood by those who preceded him. Herodotus, as we have remarked, had stated that there was a χάσμα γῆς (a deep chasm) at Colossæ, and that the Lycus flowed by a subterranean channel for half a mile. This chasm Mr. Hamilton traced, proving how the Lycus may well have been *said* to have flowed underground, owing to the great accumulation of petrifying matter from the stream, now called *Ak Sú,* or "White Water." Mr. Hamilton quotes, also, a passage from the Byzantine writer, Curopalates, clearly referring to the same curious phenomenon. Pliny, too, makes an interesting remark as to the quality of this water, where he says, "There is a river at Colossæ which will convert brick into stone." Hamilton adds, "The Ak Sú, which joins the Choruk in the centre of the town, would soon cover a brick with a thick incrustation, and even fill the porous interior with the same substance by means of infiltration."

The only towns in Galatia we think worthy of any especial note are ANCYRA, PESSINUS, and TAVIUM—in fact, Galatia, the land of the Asiatic Gauls, was little more than a dismemberment of the ancient Phrygia, mainly induced by the invasion of a portion of the vast horde of Gauls, who, descending from Pannonia under the second Brennus, B.C. 279, were, ultimately, induced to cross the Hellespont, on the invitation of Nicomedes I. of Pergamus. The general history of Galatia is so well known, we need not dwell on it here. Suffice it, that the three principal tribes of these invaders were known as the Tectosages, the Tolistoboii, and the Trocmi, and that, after many battles, in which their power was greatly reduced, they were settled, the first at Ancyra, the second at Pessinus, and the third at Tavium. Some historical facts connected with them, it may, however, be as well to mention; viz., that Antiochus obtained the name of Soter from the great defeat he inflicted on them; and that, beaten by Attalus I. and Prusias, they were most completely subdued by the consul Manlius in A.D. 189. Gauls are found as mercenaries in all the wars of the times, and, often, fighting against one another, being even noticed as such in the Maccabees (1. viii. 2). So late as the fourth century, St. Jerome, who had lived long at Trèves, states that the common tongue of Galatia was the same as that of that city. Curiously, only one name, certainly Celtic, *Eccobriga,* between Tavium and Ancyra, has been preserved in the Itineraries. As a people, they greatly resembled the Gauls Cæsar describes—"Natio est omnis Gallorum admodum dedita superstitionibus"; hence, they adopted, at once, the Phrygian worship of Cybele as "Mater Deorum,"—the "Galli" of Pessinus being her special priests. Their leading men, however, soon became wealthy, and were speedily Hellenized.

The most important place in Galatia was ANCYRA, on the Sangarius; traditionally, the foundation of Midas, the son of Gordius. The anchor he found there, whence the city's name, Pausanias says, was, still, in his day, preserved in the Temple of Jupiter. The territory round this city was formally created a Roman province by Augustus, B.C. 25, the epithet "Tectosagum" being added to its title "Sebaste," to distinguish it from Pessinus and Tavium, which bore, also, the epithets of Sebaste or Augusta. On the coins of Nero, Ancyra is, also, called Metropolis; and, though much decayed, is still a considerable place, with a large population.[105] In the adjacent plains occurred the mighty conflict between Bayazíd and Timúr (Tamerlane), in which the former lost his crown, and was taken prisoner by the Moghul emperor, though the popular legend of the "cage of Bayazíd" is, probably, as little authentic as the burning of the library of Alexandria by the orders of Omar.

105. In the Jerusalem and Antonine Itineraries we notice one name, *Ipeto-brogea*, the latter portion of which is probably Celtic, like *Allobroges*, &c.

But the most interesting matter, in connection with Ancyra is the famous Inscription of Augustus[106] (sometimes called his "Will"), generally known by scholars under the title of the "Marmor Ancyranum." What was then visible of this Inscription was first copied by Busbequius, about A.D. 1555, and published in 1579, at Antwerp, by Andreas Schottus.[107] At first, the Latin portion only was obtained, but, by degrees, portions of the Greek have been recovered, an important addition having been made by Mr. Hamilton.[108] A very complete account of it has been recently published by Theod. Mommsen, under the title "Res gestæ Divi Augusti," Berl. 1865, with very accurate copies of the Greek legend, specially executed for Napoleon III. by M. Perrot.

106. The whole town of Ancyra swarms with inscriptions. Mr. Hamilton says: "The collection of inscriptions made during my stay at Ancyra was very numerous; many of them never before published. They were met with in all parts of the town,—in the gateways and courtyards of private houses, but, chiefly, on the walls of the citadel."

107. The original inscription was engraved at Rome on brazen tablets in front of his Mausoleum (Sueton. Aug.), known in Mediæval times under the name of *L'Austa*. From an inscription in Boeckh, C. I. Gr. No. 4,039, we learn that the Ancyran inscription was placed in the Σεβαστῆον (Augusteum), and on one of the antæ of the Temple are the words—

Γαλατῶν [τ]ὁ [κοινὸν]

[ἱε] ρασάμενον

Θεῷ Σεβαστῷ

Καὶ Θεᾷ Ῥώμῃ

This is probably the temple alluded to in the decree of Augustus, and referred to by Josephus (Antiq. xvi. 6).

> 108. Too much credit cannot be given to Mr. Hamilton for his successful labours in copying the greater part of the Greek version, which in many instances supplies defects in the Latin version. "I entered," says he, "into a negotiation with the proprietor of the house ... (abutting on the Temple).... In the course of two days I had the satisfaction of finding that he had agreed to my proposal. I had hardly dared to hope that the Mahometan would have allowed a Ghiaour to take down the wall of his house for such a purpose."

It would be impossible to give here even the briefest summary of this very interesting and valuable inscription, which fully deserves the most careful perusal; but we may mention that, among the historical events Augustus records, are his crushing the murderers of Julius Cæsar, when he was only 21,—the titles conferred on him—the census of his people—the closing of the Temple of Janus—his great largesses to the people, agreeably with the will of Julius Cæsar—with a remarkable list of the monumental works begun or completed by him in Rome[109]—a notice of the highest value to Roman antiquaries, and, therefore, very properly given by Mr. Parker in his recent volume on the "Forum Romanum." He then recounts his crushing the pirates, noticing also the Servile war; the effect of the battle of Actium on Italy; the boundaries of the provinces then subject to him, and the extension of the Roman arms to Æthiopia and Arabia; the submission of Tiridates and Phraates, the kings of Parthia; and of Dubnovelaunus, king of the Britons. He concludes by saying, "When I wrote this I was in my seventy-sixth year," and very shortly after this he died.[110]

> 109. An interesting work is extant by Julius Frontinus on the Aqueducts to the city of Rome, which has been remarkably illustrated by the recent researches of Mr. J. H. Parker, C.B., on the spot; see, also, for the "Monumentum Ancyranum," J. H. Parker's "Forum Romanum and Via Sacra," Pl. xxvii.-ix.; Lond. 8vo, 1876.

> 110. Mr. Pullan gives a view of the entrance to the Temple.

The next town of Galatia we notice, PESSINUS, was situate near the left bank of the Sangarius, on the road to Angora. It was the capital of the Gallic tribe of the Tolistoboii, and celebrated in antiquity for its worship of the goddess Rhea, or Cybele. The story went that the original shrine of this goddess was removed to Rome, towards the close of the second Punic war, the safety of Italy being said to depend on this step. It is clear that the people of Pessinus did not care much about their most sacred shrine—possibly, however, as King Attalus supported the Roman demand, they could not help themselves. It is worthy of note, that, not long after the removal of this shrine, the Galli became the chief priests of the worship of Cybele, and, as such, went out to propitiate Manlius, when about to throw a bridge over the Sangarius (Livy, xxxviii. 18). Polybius gives the names of these priests (Polyb. Fragm. 4). Coins of Pessinus exhibit the worship of Cybele as late as Caracalla, and we know that Julian the Apostate visited her temple (Ammian. xxii. 9). One name she bore was that of Agdistis, Pessinus itself being seated under this mountain, which was also called Dindymus. M. Texier seems to have first recognized its ruins at a place now called Sevrihissar, of which an excellent account is given by Mr. Hamilton (i. p. 438). "Every step we advanced," says he, "gave evidence of the importance and magnificence of the public buildings with which this site must once have been adorned." We may add that Mr. Hamilton's further researches enabled him to reconcile the conflicting accounts of the march of Manlius in Polybius and Livy, the whole of the course of the Roman general being, now, fairly traceable.

The last of these Galatian towns, TAVIUM, was the abode of the third Gallic tribe, the Trocmi, as is shown by an inscription on a coin, reading ΤΑΟΥΙΑΝΩΝ ΤΡΟ. The position of this town has been identified by Mr. Hamilton as that where M. Texier found some very remarkable sculptures, which he, erroneously, called Pterium, the site of one of the battles between Crœsus and Cyrus. It is more probable that this place was much nearer the shores of the Black Sea. If Hamilton is right, Boghaz-kieui marks the site of the old town, which was one of great trade, and famous for a colossal bronze statue and temple of Jupiter. The careful measurement of the seven great roads, recorded as having met at Tavium, agrees, too, with his view. The bas-reliefs discovered by M. Texier, about two miles from this temple, are among the most curious in Asia Minor. Mr. Hamilton gives a view of them (vol. i. p. 394), whence we are inclined to think that they must be of Persian origin. So far as we can judge from the engraving, the work resembles much that at Behistan; moreover, two of the figures seem to be standing on lions or panthers, as on the reliefs found by Mr. Layard at Bavian, and to be seen, also, of some of the coins of Tarsus. The subject appears to be the meeting of two kings, the principal figures being five feet high. Two of the figures stand on a kind of double-headed eagle. Mr. Hamilton suggested a resemblance between them and those at Persepolis, an appreciation the more remarkable that when Mr. Hamilton's work was published in 1842, none of the Assyrian excavations had been begun. Considering the great influence of the Persians after the establishment of the empire of Darius, the son of Hystaspes, there is no improbability in the carving being the work of some powerful satrap, like Pharnabazus, who might easily have been familiar with the sculptures at Bavian, Behistan, and Persepolis.

Over the towns in the remaining provinces of Asia Minor, *Cappadocia, Pontus, Paphlagonia,* and *Bithynia,* it will not be necessary for us to linger at any length; not because there are not abundant objects of interest in each of them, but that the remains, purely Greek, are comparatively few, while the space we can give for an adequate description of them is exceedingly limited. We shall, however, notice some of the chief places, either of Greek origin, or directly connected with the Greeks, referring to the journals of the travellers we have so often quoted; and especially to Mr. Hamilton, for a more full and detailed account of them.

To take first *Cappadocia*, which is in this sense peculiar, that it was for centuries governed, first by satraps claiming descent from one of the seven conspirators who aided Darius, and, secondly, by a native race of kings, till it became a Roman province. The great plains of Cappadocia, at an altitude seldom less than 4,000 feet above the sea, were famous for the breed of horses they raised; corn, too, and many excellent fruits found in this province their native home. Salt, and various kinds of crystal, were also largely exported from Cappadocia.

Of the towns of Cappadocia, we may mention NAZIANZUS, a site celebrated as the birthplace of its famous bishop, Gregory, a great ecclesiastical writer, a wit and a poet (see his humorous description of Sasina, the church to which he was first appointed, Orat. xxv. p. 435, which we wish we had space to quote). Its ancient position has been accurately determined by the observations of more than one modern traveller (Hamilton, ii. p. 228). *Mazaca*, afterwards called CÆSAREA *ad Argæum*, was for many centuries the capital of Cappadocia, and is still a place of some importance. The chief feature of its scenery was the Mons Argæus (now Erjish Dagh), reputed the loftiest mountain of Asia Minor, which rises immediately above it, covered with perpetual snow. The town itself, though ultimately the capital, appears to have been for a long time little more than a camp; indeed, Horace's description probably tells us all that "His Majesty" of Cappadocia really required: "Mancipiis locuples, eget æris Cappadocum rex" ("Though rich in slaves, the king of Cappadocia lacks ready money"), (Ep. i. 6, 39). Cappadocian slaves were abundant in Rome, and had a high reputation as bakers and confectioners (Plut. Lucull. Athen. i. 20, &c.). One of the most memorable events of the history of the town was, its long and gallant resistance to the Sassanian emperor, in the war between Valerian and Sapor. In Christian times, it derived much fame from the fact that St. Basil was born there, and was, subsequently, for many years its bishop (Socrat. H. E. v. 8; Hierocl. p. 698). Mr. Hamilton (ii. pp. 274-281) gives an interesting account of his ascent of the great mountain near it [the height of which he found to be about 13,000 feet], a feat, we believe, he was the first to accomplish.

TYANA, another Cappadocian town, is chiefly noted as the birthplace of Apollonius of Tyana, whose amusing life has been preserved by Philostratus. From its position on the defiles leading through Taurus into Cilicia, it must have been a place of some importance; and hence, probably, the tradition that it was built by Semiramis (Strab. xii. 537). In later times it was the seat of a Christian bishopric (Greg. Naz. Epist. 33). Hamilton thinks that a place called *Iftyan Kas* may mark this site. There is near to it the remains of a fine aqueduct, ascribed by the natives to Nimrod, but, really, of Roman origin.

COMANA, the only other place in Cappadocia, which it is necessary to notice, was really the chief town of a subdistrict called Cataonia. It was chiefly celebrated for its collection of priests, soothsayers, and the like, who were devoted to the worship of Mâ (the Moon), or, as some say, the Cappadocian Bellona. Strabo asserts that the votaries of this sacred institution amounted to as many as 6,000 persons, of both sexes (xii. 535). Some, on the other hand, think this goddess the Anaitis of the Persians, the Agdistis or Cybele of the Phrygians. Coins of Comana, of Antoninus Pius, show that there was a Roman colony there, which was in existence as late as Caracalla.

Pontus, a narrow slip along the shores of the Black Sea, was chiefly memorable for its great fertility in the fruits now so common in our western lands, as cherries (perhaps so named from one of its towns, Cerasus), peaches, almonds, &c. It was also very rich in grain, timber, honey, and wax; while its mineral wealth is strikingly shown by the fact that one of its tribes, the Chalybes, famous so early as the time of Xenophon for their skill in working iron, gave their name to the Greek word for hardened iron or steel.[111] TRAPEZUS (now Trebisonde), its only considerable town, was in ancient days believed to be a colony of Sinope, the foundress of several other places along the coasts of the Black Sea. It was evidently a city of note when Xenophon came there, in B.C. 400, with the remains of the Ten Thousand, as its citizens hospitably entertained the Greek host under his command. We find it, also, in much prosperity when Arrian was governor of Pontus, under Hadrian. In later days, Trapezus was the capital of a petty empire under a branch of the princely house of the Comneni, its rulers assuming the pompous title of Emperors of Trebizonde, and claiming, though not always securing, independence of the Greek Empire. It is still a place of commercial importance. We may add that it was not far from this place, near the town of Zela, that Cæsar defeated the troops of the despicable traitor Pharnaces so quickly, that he announced his victory in the famous words, "Veni, Vidi, Vici" ("I came, I saw, I conquered") (Hist. Bell. Alex. c. 72; Plut. Vit. Cæs.; Sueton. Cæs. c. 37). The history of Pontus is closely interwoven with that of the famous Mithradates; but, into this, we have not the space to enter here.

111. Æschylus, Pers., v. 715, speaks of οἱ σιδηροτέκτονες Χάλυβες.

Paphlagonia is chiefly famous for the vast forests that clothed the southern and more hilly portions of its territory, and for its vast herds of horses, mules, &c. (the former of which are noticed so early as Homer (Il. ii. 281 and 852)). Its only two towns of any note were AMASTRIS, in the days of Pliny the Younger a handsome place, with squares and many public buildings,—and

SINOPE; both towns, certainly, of remote antiquity, the latter, indeed, attributed by some to the Argonauts, and by others to the Amazons. In the days of Xenophon, SINOPE was a rich and flourishing city; and then, and for a long time, subsequently, the navy of Sinope was highly distinguished among those of the other maritime cities of Greece. Sinope was also famous, like Byzantium, for the fishery of the *pelamys* or tunny-fish; deriving, also, much of its subsequent wealth from the fact, that it was selected by the kings of Pontus as their royal residence. Lucullus first, and Cæsar, subsequently, in the wars with Mithradates and Pharnaces, respectively, treated the people with much kindness, and left to them most of the works of sculpture with which their town had been embellished by the Pontic monarchs. Sinope is mentioned as a flourishing place in the times of Strabo, Trajan, and Arrian, nor did it decay, till every other place, in like manner and for the same reasons, decayed on the advent of the barbarians from Central Asia, under the hoofs of whose horses, as the proverb says, no grass ever grows again.

Bithynia, the last province of Asia Minor to which we shall have to call attention, was, as we have remarked before in the case of Mysia, in its population, largely of Thracian origin. Subsequently to Cyrus the younger, it was ruled by a series of native kings, the last of whom, Nicomedes II., bequeathed his country to the Romans. Many of these rulers were men of tried valour; thus one defeated a general of Alexander the Great; and another crushed the invading Gauls. Pliny the Younger, in his letters, gives an interesting account of the spread of Christianity in this province, at the same time showing that his stern and hardy master, Trajan, was less inclined to act severely against them than his literary and philosophic lieutenant. The towns of Bithynia to which we propose to call attention, are PRUSA, NICÆA, and NICOMEDIA.

PRUSA, generally distinguished by the epithet *ad Olympum*, more clearly to mark its site, is said to have been built by Hannibal (Plin. v. 2), but was, probably, much older, though Chrysostom, a native of the town, does not claim for it any high antiquity (Orat. xliii. p. 585). It continued to flourish under the Roman Empire (Plin. Epist. x. 35), and was, also, for a while, a leading place under the Greek Empire; indeed, it is still, under the modified name of Broussa, one of the chief cities of Turkish Anatolia. Its name will, doubtless, be fresh in the memory of many of our readers as the long home of the gallant Abd-el-Kader, and of more than one of the Hungarian leaders whom the treachery of Georgey compelled to abandon their native country. The grand Olympus which overhangs Broussa was generally termed the Mysian, to distinguish it from the Olympus of Thessaly. Near it was the town of Hadriani (now Edrenos), the coins of which bear the inscription ΑΔΡΙΑΝΕΩΝ ΠΡΟΣ ΟΛΥΜΠΙΟΝ.

NICÆA, so named after his wife by Lysimachus, was the real capital of Bithynia, and, for a long time, one of the most important towns of Western Asia. Pliny the Younger, as governor of the province, undertook to restore it, and, during the later Byzantine period it was constantly taken and retaken by the Greeks and Turks, respectively. Leake and other travellers show that there are abundant remains of this famous old town, now called Isnik; not that, under the Turks, it is, or ever could have become, a great city. In Ecclesiastical story, Nicæa will ever be memorable as the site where assembled, in A.D. 325, the grand body of bishops, so well known as the *Council of Nice*, to condemn the Arian heresy. Our own Church is believed to owe to it its most valuable "Nicene" Creed. Coins of Nicæa abound even as late as the time of Gallienus.

NICOMEDEIA, as the name implies, the chief residence of the Bithynian kings of the name of Nicomedes, was a large and flourishing city, and, as may be gathered from the letters of Pliny to Trajan, long continued so; indeed, in later times, when occupied with the Parthian or other Eastern wars, it was a convenient and constant residence for the Roman emperors (Niceph. Callist. vii.). We have a curious account of the ruin done to this city by an earthquake in one of the strange orations of Julian's friend, the orator Libanius, entitled μονῳδία ἐπὶ Νικομηδείᾳ, in which he mourns the loss of its public baths, temples, gymnasia, &c.: some of these were, however, subsequently restored by Justinian (Procop. Ædif. v. 1). The historian Arrian was born here, and Constantine the Great died at his villa Ancyron, hard by.

Having said so much on the subject of the leading Greek cities of Asia Minor, or rather of some of them, we shall notice, but as briefly as possible, the principal islands adjacent to its shores; and as the space at our disposal compels us to contract our narrative within the closest limits, we shall refer only to *Lesbos*, *Samos*, *Chios*, *Rhodus*, and *Cyprus*. *Crete*, as a matter of fact, is generally attached, geographically, to the continent of Greece, but, in any case, would require a volume to itself that adequate justice should be done to its ancient and modern story.

LESBOS, which lay off the coast of Mysia, indeed, about seven miles from Assos, was celebrated in ancient times for its high cultivation of poetry and music, and for the many men of literary eminence it produced. To Lesbos we owe Terpander and Arion of Methymna, Alcæus, and Sappho; and Pittacus, Theophrastus, and Cratippus were also born there. More than one passage in Homer, and especially Il. xx. 544, and Odyss. iv. 342, show that many of the towns in the island had large populations, even in remote times, and owned, also, a considerable extent of territory on the mainland opposite. Lesbos displayed a personal love for freedom, which contrasted well with their kinsmen on the continent; for, though crushed, for a while, by Polycrates of Samos, and submitting, perhaps, wisely, to Harpagus, the general of Cyrus, the Lesbians were among the most active seconders of the revolt of Aristagoras, suffering severely in the end, as did Chios and Tenedos, when the Persians won the day. So, too, at Salamis, they stoutly supported the Greek cause. Their subsequent history was that of most of the islands in the Ægæan. Sometimes they were for, perhaps more often against, Athens; paying often dearly enough for their love of freedom; and being, in the end, chiefly under Athens, which, while strenuously advocating the so-called sacred cause of freedom, took good care to divide their lands among her own citizens. In later days, they struggled against Roman aggrandisement, but, of course, in vain. The Romans, however, do not seem to have treated the island with severity, and, as late as Commodus, we have a coin reading KOINON Λεσβίων, which implies some amount of self-government. We may mention, incidentally, that, at Lesbos, Julius Cæsar received a civic crown for saving the life of a soldier (Livy, Epit. 87; Sueton. c. 2); that, in A.D. 802, Irene, the Byzantine empress, here ended her strange life; and, that four centuries later, John Palæologus gave Lesbos, as her dowry, to his sister, when about to marry Francis Gateluzio, in whose hands the island remained till overwhelmed by the Turks.

SAMOS, a name said to mean highland, and, doubtless, deserving this name for its far superior height to the islands adjacent, bore, like Lesbos, many different names in antiquity, with a population much intermixed, the result of successive colonies of Carians, Leleges, and Ionians. To the last people it chiefly owed its historic fame, having been, in very early times, an active member of the Ionian confederacy. As islanders, the Samians had much credit for their skill in boatbuilding; indeed, Thucydides (i. 13) goes so far as to say they were the first boatbuilders, a statement, evidently, to be accepted with a good deal of allowance. It seems, however, certain that a citizen of Samos, one Cælius, was the first to reach the Atlantic by passing through the Pillars of Hercules, and that Polycrates, the friend of Anacreon, did much to increase the naval fame of his island.

After having made treaties with Amasis of Egypt, and Cambyses of Persia (which alone show the eminence ascribed to Samos at this early period), we know further, that, from Samos, as his head-quarters, Datis sailed for Marathon, the inference being that Samos at that time was less Greek than perhaps, it ought to have been; hence too, perhaps, somewhat later, the severe punishment inflicted on it by Pericles and Sophocles. From the commencement of the Roman wars in the East, Samos seems, generally, to have sided with Rome, becoming, ultimately, part of the province of "Asia." Hence, too, probably the fact that Augustus (or rather as he then was, Octavianus) spent his winter there after the battle of Actium. Samos was, in early times, greatly devoted to the worship of Juno, and Herodotus states that her temple there was the largest he had seen. It was, however, never completely finished. According to Virgil, Samos was the second in the affections of Juno, and, in Strabo's time, in spite of the plunder it had suffered in the Mithradatic war, and, subsequently, by Verres, her temple was a complete picture-gallery. Here too, as so often elsewhere, a Sacred Way led from the temple to the city. Samos was also famous for an earthenware of a "red lustrous" character. Her art, in this respect, was copied by the Romans, their common red ware being popularly called "Samian." Of this most Museums have abundant and excellent specimens (Marryat, "Pottery and Porcelain," 1850).

CHIOS, now *Scio*, in ancient days known by the name Pityusa, referring doubtless to its abundant pine-forests, was nearly as close to the mainland of Asia Minor as Lesbos, and, in size, rather more than twice that of the Isle of Wight. It was in character peculiarly rugged, its epithet in Homer [of whom it claimed to be the birthplace], of παιπαλοέσσα (the "craggy"), being literally true. In ancient and in modern times it has been famed for the beauty of its women; in the former, also, for the excellence of its wines. In an oval place, not far from its chief town, stood the temple of Cybele, whose worship the Chiotes especially affected; and, that all things might fit properly, the careless Pococke seeing there her headless statue, which he describes as that of Homer, with equal judgment converted the lions between which she is sitting into Muses! Its present chief town is said, in situation, to resemble Genoa in miniature. Traditionally, its oldest people were the Pelasgi; but Ion, a native writer, with better reason, traces them to Crete. Chios was little injured by the first Persian conquest, as the Persians, then like Timúr, eighteen hundred years later, had no fleet; but it was thoroughly sacked and plundered, subsequently, for the crime of having sent one hundred ships to fight off Miletus in aid of the Ionians (Herod. vi. 8, 32).

During the Peloponnesian war, Chios at first supported the Athenians, but was afterwards ravaged by them, though they failed to take its capital. So, in the Mithradatic war, though at first supporting the king of Pontus, Chios fell under his displeasure, in that it had allowed Roman "negotiatores" to frequent and settle in its ports, and had to pay 2,000 talents, and to suffer still rougher treatment at the hands of his general, Zenobius. In modern times, Scio has suffered more perhaps than any other Greek island. Early in the fourteenth century, the Turks secured possession of it by a general massacre; in 1346, it was taken from them by the Genoese, who held it for nearly two centuries and a half, till it was recaptured by the Turks. In 1822, having been foolishly over-persuaded—though then a comparatively flourishing island— to join in the revolt of the Greeks against the Turks, a powerful Ottoman fleet attacked it, who, landing, massacred right and left, enslaved its women and children, and made, as is their wont, a well-cultivated district a desert, destroying, too, by fire and sword a town with thirty thousand inhabitants.

No doubt fifty-four years is a very long time in the eyes of mere politicians; but historians might have been expected to remember "Scio," and to have anticipated similar results at "Batak," or wherever else these barbarians are able to repeat the habits and practices of their fore-fathers.

RHODUS, an island about ten miles from the south-west end of Lycia, next claims our attention, as one of the most important of the Greek settlements of antiquity, and as retaining still something of its ancient splendour. In remote ages as the adopted abode of the Telchines, a celebrated brotherhood of artists, probably of Phœnician origin, Rhodes soon became famous for its cultivation of the arts, so imported, leading, as these did, naturally, to a civilization much in advance of the people around them. Its early history abounds with many legendary tales, which we regret we cannot insert here (but see Pindar Ol. vii.; Hom. Il. ii. 653). The Rhodians, no doubt from their early connections with the Phœnicians, were among the greatest navigators of antiquity, and this, too, earlier than B.C. 776, when the Olympian games are said to have been instituted: hence the foundation by them of very remote colonies in Sicily, Italy, and Spain; in the latter country, especially *Rosas*, which, remarkably enough, retains its ancient name, but slightly modified. The Rhodian code of naval laws became too, as is well known, not only the law of the Mediterranean, but the basis of the law of much more modern times. The people of this island did not, perhaps, for prudential reasons, join in the Ionian revolt or in the Persian war.

In the Peloponnesian war, too, they did not take an active part, though serving (according to Thucydides), with reluctance, on the side of Athens, against the people of Syracuse and Gela. In those days they were chiefly valued as light troops, especially, as darters and slingers. In the cause of Darius Codomannus against Alexander, the Rhodians supported Memnon, the ablest admiral of the day, whose death, perhaps more than that of any other individual person, hastened the downfall of the Persian monarchy; and somewhat subsequently, their resistance to Demetrius Poliorcetes, in the memorable siege they underwent, secured them the highest credit, and the admiration of their conqueror. Indeed, they were in such esteem among their neighbours, that (so Polybius states) when their city had been almost destroyed by an earthquake, the rulers of Sicily, Asia Minor, Syria, and Egypt vied with each other in the liberality of the supplies and presents they sent to repair this calamity. To the Romans their services were of the highest value, indeed, it was mainly due to them, that the naval operations of Livius, the Roman admiral, were successful in the wars against Philip and Antiochus (Liv. xxxi. 14; xxxvii. 9, &c.).

But, perhaps, the most interesting matter in connection with the island of Rhodes is the history of the researches recently conducted there by Messrs. Biliotti and Salzmann on the site of Camirus, one of the three chief original cities of that island, the combining of which together, about B.C. 408, resulted in the creation of the capital city, Rhodes. It was natural, therefore, to expect that any antiquities discovered at these places would be earlier than this date. The ground all round is now covered by a pine forest, in the clearing of which the old necropolis was discovered by a bullock falling into a tomb. In 1853, Mr. Newton obtained many *terra-cotta* vases of a very archaic type, and other fictile vases from the peasants' houses of the adjacent village of Kalaverda. Some of the *pinakes* or platters, with geometrical patterns painted in brown on a pale ground, resembled the oldest objects of this class from the tombs of Athens and Melos; the sites, too, of Mycenæ and Tiryns are also strewn with similar fragments.[112] Other amphoræ and oinochoæ, with black figures on a red ground, or red figures on a black, were also met with.[113]

112. As has been well shown in Dr. Schliemann's recent researches.

113. Travels in the Levant, i. p. 235.

Shortly after this, a *firman* was obtained from Constantinople, empowering Messrs. Biliotti and Salzmann to make a thorough investigation into this ancient site, the result of which has been the opening of at least 275 tombs. From these tombs many precious works of art in gold, bronze, and glass, with figures in terra-cotta, and calcareous stones, together with vases and alabaster jars, have been procured, some of them probably as old as B.C. 650. The whole may be grouped under the heads: (1) Asiatico-Phœnician, or Archaic Greek; (2) Greek of the best and latest periods; (3) Egyptian, or imitations of Egyptian. The first is the most important, as comprehending most of the gold and silver ornaments, with a few terra-cottas. It has been supposed that the makers of these objects were Phœnicians of Tyre and Sidon; but, as many of the specimens betray a marked Assyrian character and influence, they are more probably copies, at second hand, of works originally Assyrian.

On examining these curious works of art, it will be observed that most of those in gold have been used either as necklaces or for attachment to other substances, probably leather, consisting, as they do, for the most part, of thin pieces or plaques of metal, averaging from one to two and a half inches in length, with subjects on them worked up, as a rule, from behind, after the fashion now called *repoussée* work. Thus we meet with standing female figures, draped to the feet (which are close together), as on the sculptures from Branchidæ, with long and elaborately-dressed hair falling on their shoulders and naked breasts, the arms being raised in a stiff and formal manner, and the hands partially closed. Another figure has large wings, almost like a *nimbus*, hands crossed, and elbows square; and against the body of this figure, a rudely-executed animal. A third holds in each hand a small lion by the tail, just as on some of the sculptures from Khorsabad. On a fourth the lions are not held, but are springing up against the figure.

On another plaque we have nearly the same type, with this distinction, that the lions stand out in very high relief, and, curiously enough, are in style almost identical with those on a *fibula* obtained from Cervetri by the late Mr. Blayds. Many instances may be seen of the *narsingh*, or man-lion type—a compound figure, with the head, body, and legs of a man, but attached to or behind this body, and, as it were, growing out of it, the body of an animal with hoofs. This monstrous form occurs, also, on a vase from Athens and on Assyrian cylinders. There are, also, specimens of winged, man-headed lions, their wings being thrown back so as to cover the whole figure, just as on the Assyrian sculptures. In some cases, we find bronze plated with gold, the latter having often been forced asunder by the rust and consequent expansion of the bronze.

Besides these objects, were found, also, small glass vessels of a rich purple colour with yellow bands, like those from Cære and other of the oldest cities of Italy, and a coffin, 6 feet 4 inches long, and 2 feet 1 inch wide, made entirely of *terra-cotta*. There are traces of brown and red paint over the whole of it, and, at one end, lions in red, with floral ornaments, and, at the other, a black bull between two brown lions. Many large terra-cotta plates were also found, with various subjects; such as the combat between Hector and Menelaus over the body of Euphorbus, with the names of the combatants written over them, a drawing of especial interest, from the archaic type of the superinscribed characters: there were, too, a Gorgon's head, sirens, and other strange animals, and a sphinx and a bull with his horns drawn in perspective. These plates were probably of local manufacture. But, besides these curious antique monuments, the excavations at Camirus brought to light many objects of very fine work, two of which must be mentioned. One, a small gold vessel of exceeding beauty, about an inch in diameter, at one end of which is a seated Eros or Cupid; on the other, Thetis on a dolphin, with the arrows Vulcan had forged for her son Achilles. The other, a magnificent amphora, with figures in red on a black ground, the subject being "the surprise of Thetis by Peleus"; in fact, the same as that on one side of the Portland vase; thus confirming, in a most unexpected manner, the interpretation originally proposed many years ago by Mr. Millingen. This vase is of the time of Alexander the Great, and few, if any vases have as yet been found in the Archipelago exhibiting such free and masterly drawing as this one from Camirus.

The island of CYPRUS, which lay off the southern coast of Asia Minor, was one of the most celebrated of those generally called the Greek Islands, though it had, probably, less claim to this designation, and was more Oriental than any of the others. It was, as was natural from its position, early settled by the Phœnicians, Herodotus speaking of the inhabitants as a very mixed race. It is not possible to determine which of several of its towns was the most ancient; but, in the early Jewish Scriptures, we read of "ships of Chittim," probably those of Citium, one of its chief towns. In later days, Paphos, itself of remote antiquity, became the capital of the island, and the residence, as we learn from the Acts of the Apostles, of the Roman proconsul. As the centre of the worship of Venus, which is noticed so early as Homer, as well as by many later writers, Paphos was greatly visited by strangers, among whom Tacitus mentions, particularly, the Emperor Titus, when on his way to besiege Jerusalem (Hist. ii. 3-4). Her symbol, or idol, was a purely Asiatic type, and consisted merely of an upright, conical, and unsculptured stone. The history of the island was a very chequered one, and there were but comparatively short intervals of time when it was really under its own native rulers; more frequently it was held by one or other of the continental empires near it which happened for the time to be the most powerful. Thus it was, usually, in the hands of the Persians, till the overthrow of that power by Alexander, when it was secured by the Ptolemies, in whose diadem it was the most precious jewel. In the end it was, of course, seized by the Romans, becoming first an Imperial province, and then, by the arrangement of Augustus, directly under the Senate. In later times, it was the seat of a bishopric, one of the most famous of the bishops of Paphos being the celebrated Epiphanius. During the Crusades, Richard Cœur de Lion captured the island and gave it to Guy de Lusignan, king of Jerusalem, whence the title of kings of Cyprus and Jerusalem, adopted, till recent times, by some of the monarchs of Western Europe.

In recent times, the Island of Cyprus has proved one of the most abundant sources of precious remains of antiquity, excavated chiefly by Mr. R. H. Lang and General Palma di Cesnola. The former gentleman has published in the Numismatic Chronicle (vol. xi. New Series, 1870), an account of the silver coins, many of native Cypriote manufacture, he lighted on while digging out an ancient temple at Dali (Idalium), in 1869. The coins were found at two several times, and, from the way in which some of them adhered together, had probably been enclosed in a bag, though no traces of it were detected. Mr. Lang believed he could trace from them the existence of the six or seven distinct kingdoms, which we know, from other sources, once existed in this island. The earliest of these coins are, perhaps, as old as the middle of the sixth century B.C.

The most important results of Mr. Lang's excavations in this temple are now in the British Museum, and have been described by him in a paper read before the Royal Society of Literature (see Transactions, New Series, vol. xi. pt. i. 1875). In this memoir, which has been supplemented with some careful observations by Mr. R. S. Poole, Mr. Lang has given many interesting details of his excavations. His first diggings were in 1868, when his men soon "came upon (as it were) a mine of statues," several of them being of colossal proportions, and on two large troughs, in an outer court, perhaps once employed for the ablutions connected with the temple, which was completely "full of the heads of small statues, which, after being broken from their bodies, had been pitched pell-mell into the troughs." Near these troughs were three rows of statues; some, too, of the chambers excavated were also full of statuary—and in a stratum of charcoal were comminuted fragments of the bones and teeth of several animals; as of bullocks, sheep, camels, and swine. We can only add, here, that the treatment of the beard on some of the heads is remarkably Assyrian; which, indeed, might reasonably have been expected, as the island was long subject to that empire,—and, that, besides coins and sculptures, Mr. Lang procured, also, several Phœnician inscriptions, not, however, of very early date, their characters being nearly identical with those on the well-known inscription in the Bodleian Library at Oxford, together with one bilingual inscription in Cypriote and Phœnician writing. The last has proved of great value, in that it enabled the late Dr. Brandis and Mr. G. Smith to settle many important points in connection with the Cyprian alphabet.

Nearly about the same time as Mr. Lang, General di Cesnola, the American consul in Cyprus, was commencing a series of excavations, the latest results of which have, in some respects, far surpassed anything Mr. Lang achieved. M. Cesnola began digging, we believe, first about 1867; but his first important discoveries were in the spring of 1870, when he found at Golgos the remains of two temples of Venus, nearly on the spot where, some time before, the Count de Vogüé had been less fortunate. It was here that M. di Cesnola formed his first collection, now for the most part in the museum of New York. As in the case of Mr. Lang, the statues had all been thrown down and grievously defaced by "iconoclastic" hands. Among them, however, were many which had been simply hurled from their pedestals, and were, therefore, nearly as fresh as when first made. One great interest in the collection is, that it is almost wholly the product of local artists. Naturally there was in it a large number of statuettes of Venus, of vases, of lamps, and of objects in glass; the latter, we believe, chiefly from Idalium. It is said that altogether there were nearly 10,000 objects, and that New York secured them for about £1 apiece. We cannot discuss here the question, much mooted at the time, whether or not the collection ought to have been bought by the English Government; but, had it been, we do not know where it could have been adequately exhibited. The British Museum seems to be as full as ever; nor is there any apparent hope of the removal of the hideous black sheds between the columns in the front of it, which have now, for these twenty years, defaced any architectural beauty it may be supposed to have.

But by far the most remarkable of General di Cesnola's discoveries are his most recent ones, the great results of which are now, we believe, on their way to New York, the American Government having had the good sense to supply him with ample means for continuing his researches in the best manner. These last, commenced in 1873, have been prosecuted at various ancient sites, such as those of Golgos, Salamis, Palæo-Paphos, Soli, and Amathus; Curium having ultimately proved the most valuable mine of antiquities. Besides two superb sarcophagi he had previously secured, M. Cesnola found at Curium a mosaic pavement, in style, as he calls it, Assyrio-Egyptian, which had already been partly dug through by some former excavator, and beneath this, at a depth of twenty feet, a subterranean passage in the rock leading into three chambers, communicating the one with the other. In the first of these he came upon a great number of small ornaments, rings, &c., in pure gold; in the second, on a considerable collection of gilt vases, cups, &c.; and in the third, on innumerable miscellaneous objects, comprising vases of alabaster, candelabra, metal mirrors, daggers, armlets, small statues of animals, &c. The most valuable individual specimens would seem to be a crystal vase and a pair of armillæ in gold, bearing a double Cypriote inscription. What then is the history of this precious *trouvaille*? We venture to think that General di Cesnola's idea on the subject is probably the true one,—that it represents the offerings in a temple now destroyed, and hurriedly packed away, possibly when it was attacked by iconoclasts. Some of the bijoux are inscribed with the names of the owners, and probably donors. Like the relics from Cameirus, these Cypriote monuments are of great antiquarian value, as proving the transition from Eastern to Greek art.

[For further details, see Atti d. Real. Acad. d. Scien. di Torino, vol. x.; and Ceccaldi, Le ultime Scoperte nell' isola di Cipro, 1876.]

CHAPTER V.

ST. PAUL.

DURING previous parts of this work we have, from time to time, alluded to the presence of St. Paul at various places we have described; the interest, however, every one feels in the great Apostle of the Gentiles induces us to throw together in one chapter a brief summary of his journeys in Asia Minor; the more so, that to a Christian, studying the history of this portion of Western Asia, St. Paul stands out alone—"none but himself can be his parallel."

St. Paul's missionary labours commenced from the period when the Holy Ghost said, "Separate me Barnabas and Paul for the work whereunto I have called them" (Acts xiii. 2); an order, doubtless, given at Antioch in Syria, as they soon after started from Seleucia, the port of Antioch, for Cyprus, the native home of Barnabas. Antioch was then the capital of Northern Syria, and as much, if not more than Jerusalem, the centre of Christian evangelization. Hence, the natural reason why at Antioch men were "first called Christians." Seleucia, too, at the mouth of the Orontes, about twenty miles below Antioch, was the "key of Syria," and had, recently, obtained from Pompey the title of a "Free City," an honour which it long retained. Dr. Yates (long a resident in the neighbourhood), in an interesting memoir on this city (in the Museum of Classical Antiquities), mentions that the names of the piers at the mouth of its harbour still preserve a record of St. Paul's voyage, the southern one being called after him, and the northern after Barnabas. Structures so vast as these may easily have remained to the present day, for Pococke states that some of the stones "are twenty feet long by five deep and six wide, and fastened together by iron cramps." The voyage from Seleucia to Cyprus is, generally, short and easy.

The first place they made in the island was Salamis,[114] whence they proceeded right across it to Paphos, the residence of the Roman governor, Sergius Paulus, "a prudent man." Here we have the remarkable story of Elymas the sorcerer, and of the conversion of the governor on witnessing the miracle by the hand of St. Paul. Cyprus was at that time, as may be gathered from Dio Cassius, under the direct government of the Emperor of Rome, together with Syria and Cilicia; but, a little later, this historian adds that Augustus restored it to the Senate. St. Luke's title, therefore, of proconsul is correct, as that invariably given to the rulers of the provinces belonging to the Senate. A Cyprian inscription in Boeckh confirms this view. The occurrence of a person called a "sorcerer" at the court of the Roman governor is quite in accordance with the manners of the times. Thus, Juvenal sarcastically speaks of the "Orontes flowing into the Tiber."[115]

114. Salamis was on the east side of the island, nearly opposite to Syria; and, in early times, the capital of the island. It was destroyed by the Romans, but rebuilt with the name of Constantia. It was a little to the north of Famagousta, the name of which, curiously enough, is not of Latin origin, as might be supposed, but a lineal descendant of the original Assyrian Ammochosta.

115. Juven. Sat. iii. 60; ib. vi. 584, 589; Horat. Od. i. xi.; Sat. ii. 1; and Juven. iii. 13, and vi. 542, point out the number of Jewish impostors of the lowest kind with whom Rome was then infested: Juvenal, vi. 553, indicates the influence the so-called Chaldean astrologers possessed there.

It has been often thought that, from the miracle over Elymas, dates the change of the name of the apostle from Saul to Paul, and certain it is that, subsequently to the words "Then Saul (who is also called Paul)" (Acts xiii. 9), the first name does not occur again; moreover, in his fourteen Epistles the apostle invariably calls himself Paul. So happened it in earlier days, when Abram was changed into Abraham. It has been further supposed that, as Barnabas was a native of Cyprus, the apostles were induced to visit that island first; but, for their crossing to Attalia in Pamphylia, in preference to any other port, no reason can be assigned, though we may conjecture that they acted on information obtained in Cyprus. The communication was no doubt easy and probably constant. Attalia, as we have pointed out, was then, as now, a place of some consequence, and almost the only port of southern Asia Minor: thence they proceeded up the steep and rugged defiles of the Pamphylian mountains to Perga, and, ultimately, to Antiochia in Pisidia. The sacred writer records no event on their route thither, except the secession of Mark, which probably took place soon after they had landed; nor has he even given the reason that influenced Mark; but this may have been as Matthew Henry has suggested: "Either he (Mark) did not like the work, or he wanted to go and see his mother." St. Paul, we know, felt acutely, what he might fairly have considered as little short of a desertion; indeed, this secession led, as we shall see hereafter, to the separation between himself and Barnabas on the eve of his second missionary journey.

Whatever Mark's reasons, certain it is he did depart, and that St. Paul pushed on with characteristic bravery through a country the nature of which we have described when speaking of Cremna, Sagalassus, and of the probable position of Perge; and which may be comprehended, in all its fulness, by those who have time to study the valuable researches of Leake and Hamilton, Spratt and Forbes, Arundell and Sir Charles Fellows. It has been reasonably conjectured that, St. Paul travelling, as he probably did a little before the full heat of the summer had commenced, attached his small party to some large group or caravan travelling inwards and northwards in the same direction. Many travellers, and especially Sir Charles Fellows, have pointed out the annual custom prevailing among the dwellers along the southern shores of Asia Minor, of leaving their homes at the beginning of the hot weather, and of migrating with their cattle and household property to the cooler valleys of the mountains.

With regard to Antioch in Pisidia, we have already shown that Mr. Arundell was the first to point out that some ruins, now called Yalobatch, can scarcely be any other than those of this Antioch. We need not, therefore, dwell any longer on this point, simply adding, that, from its great commercial importance, St. Paul must have found there many resident Jews, while we know that there was at least one synagogue.

On arriving at Antioch, the narrative in the Bible goes on to say that the Apostles "went into the synagogue on the Sabbath-day, and sat down"; then, after the reading the Law, as was and still is, the usual custom, the rulers of the synagogue desired them to speak, and St. Paul gave one of his most characteristic addresses, being, at first, well received by his own countrymen, and, especially so, by those persons who, having given up idol-worship, were usually known as proselytes. He was, therefore, invited to preach on the following Sabbath-day, the intervening week having been, no doubt, well employed in constant meetings between St. Paul and these proselytes, and in earnest addresses and exhortations. Hence, we are told that, on this second occasion, "came almost the whole city together to hear the word of God." But this was more than the Jews could endure: so they stirred up the "chief men of the city," and the Apostles were soon after (we are not told how soon) "expelled out of their coasts," that is, ordered to go beyond the limits of the Roman colony of Antioch; though, as they returned to it again, shortly afterwards, it is likely that no formal decree of banishment was promulgated against them. On this "they shook off the dust of their feet against them."[116]

> 116. The action used by the Apostles was, it will be remembered, in obedience to the direct words of our Lord: "Whosoever," said He, "shall not receive you nor hear you, when ye depart thence, shake off the dust under your feet as a testimony against them" (Matt. x. 14; Mark vi. 11; Luke ix. 5). It was, in fact, a symbolical act, implying that the city was regarded as profane. It may be presumed that the "devout and honourable women" (Acts xiii. 50) were proselytes.

St. Paul's speech, on the second Sabbath, is worthy of note as that in which he first definitely stated the object of his mission; for, when thus attacked by his own countrymen, he turned upon them with the words, "It was necessary that the word of God should first have been spoken to you; but, seeing ye put it from you and judge yourselves unworthy of everlasting life, we turn to the Gentiles" (Acts xiii. 46). Strabo (vii. 3) has pointed out that "feminine influence" was a remarkable characteristic of the manners of Western Asia in his day, and of this we find the Jews availing themselves, on this occasion. Leaving Antioch, then, the Apostles turned nearly south-east to Iconium, which, as we have already stated, was, in those days, the chief town of the sub-district of Lycaonia. The treatment the Apostles received at Iconium was not very different from that they had experienced at Antioch. Here, as there, "the unbelieving Jews stirred up the Gentiles," but were not, for some time, successful in their designs, as the Apostles were able to abide there a long time, "speaking boldly in the Lord." In fact, as at Ephesus, "the multitude of the city was divided, and part held with the Jews, and part with the Apostles" (xiv. 4). In the end, however, the Jews prevailed: so the Apostles had to save themselves from being stoned, by flight "unto Lystra and Derbe, cities of Lycaonia, and unto the region that lieth round about" (ver. 6), "and there," it is added, "they preached the Gospel."

We have, already, shown that there is some doubt as to the position of these two towns, but that Mr. Falkener has probably found Lystra on the side of a mountain called Karadagh, at a place called by the Turks Bin-bir-Kalessi, or, the Thousand Churches. So, too, the site of Derbe has, certainly, not been yet made out completely; but, from the similarity of name, it may be at Divle, as suggested by Hamilton.

The narrative of what took place at Lystra is very interesting. At first, we may presume that St. Paul preached to any chance groups that collected around him: after some time, however, he saw a poor cripple "who had never walked," and "perceiving that he had faith to be healed," at once cured him, saying to him with a loud voice, "Stand upright on thy feet." Need we wonder that the astonishment of the people vented itself in the natural exclamation that "the gods had come to us in the likeness of men." The narrative implies the existence, before the walls of the city, of a temple of Jupiter (Acts xiv. 13), some traces of which may, perhaps, still remain, and, if so, will serve, hereafter, for the identification of the site. Messrs. Conybeare and Howson have pointed out that the beautiful legend of the visit of Jupiter and Mercury to the earth, in Ovid's story of Baucis and Philemon, belongs to this part of Asia Minor: the people of Lystra would, therefore, have been prepared to recognize in Barnabas and Paul the Jupiter and Mercury of their own fables. What was the "speech of Lycaonia" we have no means of telling, no undoubted words of this dialect having, so far as we are aware, been preserved.

But the Lycaonians, though, at first, so readily convinced of the divinity of the Apostles, soon showed themselves as fickle as the "foolish Galatians." St. Luke adding, "and there came thither certain Jews from Antioch and Iconium and persuaded the people, and having stoned Paul, drew him out of the city, supposing that he was dead," so little lasting was the impression produced, even by the cure of one born a cripple. It is, doubtless, to this attack upon him that St. Paul, subsequently, alludes in the words, "Once was I stoned" (2 Cor. xi. 25). That he was not killed, like St. Stephen, as Barnabas and his friends feared and the Jews hoped, is a miracle in itself. Any how, he recovered at once as "he rose up and came into the city," and departed next day "with Barnabas to Derbe." It was at Lystra that St. Paul made the acquaintance of Timotheus (or Timothy) his future constant and steadfast companion. With Derbe ends all that has been recorded of St. Paul's First journey. On the return, however, of Paul and Barnabas, we learn that they fearlessly visited again all the places where they had previously preached, "confirming the souls of the disciples, and exhorting them to continue in the faith." At the same time, too, they ordained "elders in every church," praying with fasting, and commending "them to the Lord, on whom they believed."

The course of the Second missionary journey of St. Paul, most of which falls within the limits of this volume, was probably determined on when the Council of the Apostles at Jerusalem sent letters "unto the brethren which are of the Gentiles in Antioch, in Syria, and in Cilicia" (xv. 23): it was manifestly, also, St. Paul's own desire, for he says, "Let us go again and visit our brethren in every city, where we have announced the word of the Lord, and see how they do." It was, on the proposal of this second journey, that the famous dispute took place between St. Paul and Barnabas, the former refusing to take with him Barnabas's kinsman Mark, because he had turned back before. For this journey (at Attalia), therefore, "Paul chose Silas, and departed, being recommended by the brethren unto the grace of God; and he went through Syria and Cilicia confirming the Churches" (ver. 40). We cannot discuss here the circumstances of this quarrel between the two "servants of the Lord," but one good result from it was, clearly, a far wider preaching of the Gospel than might otherwise have occurred; as, by this separation, two distinct streams of missionary labour were provided instead of one; Barnabas taking the insular, while St. Paul took the continental line.

We do not know which way St. Paul went on leaving Antioch, but it is most likely he passed into Cilicia by the "Syrian Gates," now called the pass of Beilan, the character of which may be fully learnt from Mr. Ainsworth and other travellers. For some unknown reason, Sacred history does not give the name of a single place visited during this confirmatory tour, till the Apostles reached Derbe and Lystra; though we may feel sure, especially as the "Gentiles of Cilicia" are mentioned in the letter of the Apostles, that St. Paul did not fail to visit his native town, Tarsus, the "no mean city" of his address to the Roman governor. At Tarsus, if anywhere in Cilicia, Christians would be surely found who would be glad of the Apostle's "confirming" words. From Tarsus, St. Paul must have passed from S.E. to N.W., through the great mountain barrier which separates the central table-land of Asia Minor from the plain country in which Tarsus was situated. There are several passes; the nearest to Tarsus and most direct, being that of the "Cilician Gates," a remarkable cleft, about eighty miles in length. Ascending, probably, by this pass, St. Paul would reach the plains of Lycaonia, at an altitude of about 4,000 feet above the sea, in four or five days. At Lystra (probably) he met again the young disciple Timotheus, "who was well reported of at Lystra and Iconium," and who, at St. Paul's request, at once joined him: thence, "as they went through the cities they delivered them the decrees for to keep that were ordained by the Apostles and Elders that were at Jerusalem; and so were the churches established in the faith, and increased in number daily." We are not told that, on this occasion, St. Paul met with any serious opposition.

The brevity of the account of this journey is most disappointing, as we do not know whether St. Paul visited even Antioch in Pisidia: all we learn is that he was *ordered* to "go through Phrygia and the region of Galatia," altogether new ground, and representing districts that could not have been evangelized before. Yet even here the names of no towns are recorded till he gets to Mysia: on the other hand, he was *not permitted* to preach the "word" in Asia; that is, within Roman "Asia," nor to enter Bithynia. Most likely, as suggested by Messrs. Conybeare and Howson, he followed the great Roman lines of communication, and passed by Laodicea, Philomelium, and Synnada.

It has been inferred from his use of the plural, "to the churches of Galatia," as the heading of his Epistle to that people, that there was no one great church there, as at Ephesus or Corinth; but this seems to us refining too much. We may, however, suppose that no special miracles marked this journey, or, at all events, none which St. Luke thought it necessary to notice. We learn from St. Paul himself (Galat. iv. 13) that it was owing to bodily sickness that he preached to the Galatians in the first instance, it may be, as has been suggested, on his way to Pontus, from which distant province we know that some Jewish proselytes had come to Jerusalem, and were present on the day of Pentecost (Acts ii. 11): moreover, it is certain, from his Epistle to the Galatians, that he had been well received by this inconstant people, a large and mixed multitude having embraced Christianity.

As, in so many other instances, no clue is given us as to the further route actually taken by the Apostles to Troas, but, by the Divine prohibition to them of preaching in "Asia," we may conjecture that the time was not ripe for spreading the Gospel among the great cities of Ephesus, Smyrna, or Pergamus. It will be noticed that the Apostles are not forbidden to *enter* Asia, as was the case with Bithynia, but only not to *preach there*. Indeed, they could not, easily, have got to Troas without passing through "Asia."

The first seaport St. Paul reached must have been Adramyttium, which is not, however, noticed here by name, though it is subsequently, when on the voyage to Rome. Of this place we have, already, given some account: and hence, it would seem, that the Apostle passed onwards to Assos and Alexandria Troas, where the remarkable vision appeared to him which is thus described:—

"And a vision appeared to Paul in the night. There stood a man of Macedonia and prayed him, saying, Come over into Macedonia, and help us. And, after he had seen the vision, immediately we endeavoured to go into Macedonia, assuredly gathering that the Lord had called us for to preach the Gospel unto them. Therefore, loosing from Troas we came with a straight course to Samothrace...." (Acts xvi. 9, 10, 11).

Compelled as we are here to compress as much as possible what must be said, we reluctantly desist from following St. Paul to Europe. We need, therefore, only state that, after two years St. Paul returned to Antioch in Syria and Jerusalem, passing, on his way, sufficient time at Ephesus, so that "he himself entered into the synagogue, and reasoned with the Jews" (xviii. 19), promising, at the request of the congregation, that he would return to Ephesus, "if God will." Having "saluted the Church" (probably of Jerusalem) he returned to Antioch, and thence "departed and went over all the country of Galatia and Phrygia in order, strengthening all the disciples,"[117] arriving, ultimately, at Ephesus, where he found Apollos, "an eloquent man, and mighty in the Scriptures" (xviii. 24).

> [117]. The brief statement in the Acts does not tell us anything of the course St. Paul took on this occasion; but as he went "over all the country of Galatia and Phrygia in order," we can have no doubt that his visitation of the churches was complete, and that he went to all or most of the places noticed in the previous journeys.

The visit of St. Paul to Ephesus was the period when it pleased God to do for the later disciples what had been previously done, twelve or thirteen years before, on the day of Pentecost: "the Holy Ghost came on them, and they spake with tongues, and prophesied." In the present instance, it is enough to refer to the words in the narrative as given in the Acts xix. 2: "He" (St. Paul) "said unto them, Have ye received the Holy Ghost since ye believed? And they said unto him, We have not so much as heard whether there be any Holy Ghost," &c.... "When they heard this, they were baptized in the name of the Lord Jesus; and when Paul laid his hands upon them, the Holy Ghost came on them, and they spake with tongues, and prophesied."

At Ephesus St. Paul dwelt more than two years, diligently preaching the Gospel, and "disputing daily in the school of one Tyrannus." No opposition appears to have arisen for some time; indeed, for three months, he was allowed the use of even the synagogue; but, in the end, the idol-brokers felt their trade was in jeopardy, and, especially, men, who, like Demetrius, the silversmith, making the "silver shrines for Diana, brought no small gain unto the craftsmen."

As at Corinth, St. Paul at Ephesus was brought, face to face, with Asiatic superstition, withstanding even magic arts, as Moses did, Jannes, and Jambres, and, also, "exorcists." What this "magic" really was has been much debated. Anyhow, the Talmud tells us that a "knowledge of magic" was required as a necessary qualification for a seat in the Sanhedrin, so that the councillor might be able to try those accused of such practices, though some of these need not, necessarily, have been of evil intention: it is clear, however, from the case of Sceva (xix. 14), that many of the "exorcists" made a bad use of any superior knowledge they possessed or pretended to have. St. Paul's success, however, in putting down this species of knavery, was so complete, that a large number of the exorcists submitted to him, and burnt their books, which were valued at a very high price. The "town-clerk" was, doubtless, as we have remarked before, a Roman officer, and, as the keeper of the public records, one of the most important personages in the town. His language in putting down the *émeute* in the theatre clearly shows this; but, as he evidently refers to others of greater power than himself, we hardly think, as some have done, that he was himself one of the "Asiarchs," or, as our translation has it, "chiefs of Asia." His language shows that he was not unfriendly to St. Paul (though not necessarily that he was, himself, a Christian); and, further, that he well knew how to deal with a multitude, "the more part of whom knew not wherefore they were come together."

We have now brought nearly to an end the short outline we felt it necessary to give of St. Paul's journeying in Asia Minor. It is probable that, soon after the disturbance in the theatre, he left for Macedonia; so that the rest of his connection with Asia Minor or with the Greek islands may be summed up in a few words. After some time passed in Macedonia, with a possible journey through Illyricum and Western Greece, which occupied him for three months (xx. 3), St. Paul returned to the north, and, passing by Philippi and Neapolis, crossed the Ægæan to Alexandria Troas. This second visit to Troas is chiefly notable for the story of the boy Eutychus, who, overcome with sleep when St. Paul continued his speech until midnight, fell to the ground and was killed. It will be observed, that, in the miracle of his restoration to life, St. Paul implied the use of the very words of our Saviour to the young maiden: "She is not dead, but sleepeth." Thence he proceeded alone on foot twenty miles to Assos, through a district then, as now, richly wooded, but with a good Roman road, long since in utter decay. It was a lonely walk the great Apostle pursued then; but solitude is sometimes required to give greater strength.

From Assos St. Paul took ship to Mytilene, proceeding onwards to Chios, Samos, Trogyllium, and Miletus. At this last place, he summoned the elders from Ephesus, and bade a solemn farewell to the Christians of Asia, among whom he had laboured so long and so efficiently; and passing thence by Coos and Rhodes to Patara, finally entered a ship there, and sailed to Phœnicia (xxi. 1). At Trogyllium the Admiralty chart shows a harbour that still bears the name of St. Paul's Port. So far as we know, with the exception of touching at Cnidus on his last voyage to Rome, St. Paul had no further connection with Asia Minor.

www.ingramcontent.com/pod-product-compliance
Ingram Content Group UK Ltd.
Pitfield, Milton Keynes, MK11 3LW, UK
UKHW031337260325
456749UK00002B/378